KIDS
IN THE
WILD
GARDEN

BY ELIZABETH MCCORQUODALE

**black dog
publishing**
london uk

CONTENTS

What do you get when you cross a lunchbox with a necklace?

A food chain!

INTRODUCTION

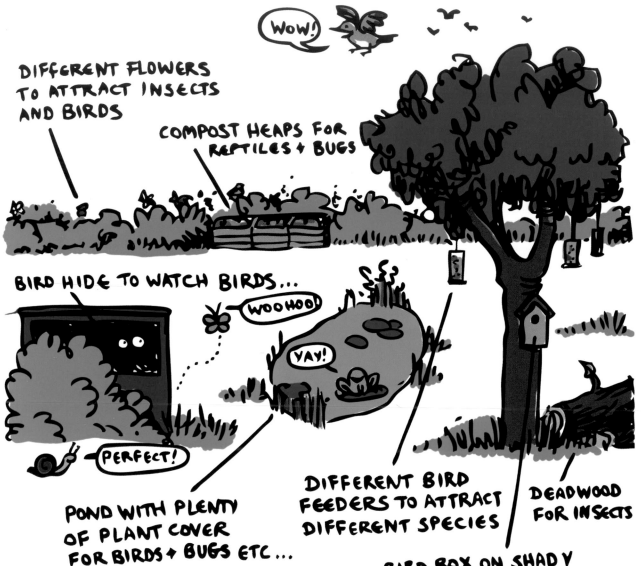

WOW!

DIFFERENT FLOWERS TO ATTRACT INSECTS AND BIRDS

COMPOST HEAPS FOR REPTILES + BUGS

BIRD HIDE TO WATCH BIRDS...

WOOHOO!

YAY!

PERFECT!

POND WITH PLENTY OF PLANT COVER FOR BIRDS + BUGS ETC...

DIFFERENT BIRD FEEDERS TO ATTRACT DIFFERENT SPECIES

DEADWOOD FOR INSECTS

BIRD BOX ON SHADY SIDE OF TREE

YOUR WILDLIFE GARDEN IS YOUR VERY OWN NATURE RESERVE; ONE THAT YOU CAN VISIT ANY TIME YOU WANT.

WHY GARDEN FOR WILDLIFE?

Why garden for wildlife? Well, because it's fun and interesting and busy. There's always something to see and something to do and there's always some cool new thing to be discovered or investigated. Gardens never stay the same and wildlife gardens have even more to grab you than ordinary gardens!

To enjoy wildlife in the garden you first need to make a garden that attracts the widest variety of birds and beasts possible. The trick, and the fun, is to grow different things and create different habitats while growing stuff that you like growing.

Naturalists have discovered that some habitats provide perfect conditions for a large number of creatures, while others are quite poor at encouraging wildlife to visit. What we want to do is to invite creatures into our gardens to feed and to breed.

Make a pond or a bog, even a small one; plant a bush or a tree; grow some nectar-rich flowers; let a corner of the lawn grow tall and collect some old logs and leave them to rot down into a lovely woody tower block which will provide a home and dining table for all kinds of creatures. There are lots of ideas in the following pages with plenty of detailed instruction, hints and tips so that you can create a terrific garden for wildlife!

IT'S A JUNGLE OUT THERE

You can have a very pretty garden, even a super vegetable plot, that is more wildlife-friendly than a whole field of wild plants, it all depends on what you grow and how you tend it.

Some people think that a wild garden has to be messy and full of brambles and nettles, but this isn't true at all. It is true that there are some butterflies that will only lay their eggs on stinging nettles, and a thicket of bramble will provide a wonderfully safe shelter for birds and small mammals to nest in; however, there are lots of other dense, thorny plants that will do the same job and be pretty at the same

time; and the countryside isn't short on nettle patches—just look at any roadside or abandoned lot.

With more people in the world than ever before, and more factories and cars and other things that take up space and create pollution, some animals and plants are finding themselves homeless. You can help to give them a new home and feed them and keep them safe by making a terrific garden that gives them what they need in the way of food and shelter, while giving you the great feeling that you are doing something good and enjoying yourself at the same time. What could be nicer!

what do you get when you cross a four-leaf clover with a stinging nettle? A rash of good luck!

HOW TO BE A WILDLIFE GARDENER

WHAT IS GOOD FOR WILDLIFE?

Plants! Everything in the whole wide world relies on plants. If there were no plants, there would be no you or me, or any other living thing. Plants provide the oxygen that we breathe and the food that is at the beginning of all food chains.

Birds, bees and butterflies are the creatures that most people think of when they think of wildlife gardening and the thing these three groups have in common are wildflowers. The nectar and pollen from flowers is the food of both bees and butterflies. Without nectar, the sugary syrup that flowers make to tempt them in, the bees and butterflies would starve to death. Without the seeds that develop inside the flowers, many birds would be unable to live through the winter or feed their young in the spring. **Flowers** are where it all starts.

Long grass is great for a whole variety of different creatures. Butterflies, bees and bugs feed on the different flowering plants that thrive among the grasses, and these attract other creatures that feed on them! Just by having a section of long grass in your garden you could invite in lizards, birds and a myriad of insects and butterflies.

But short grass is very handy for playing on and for having picnics on, and, let's face it, adults are strangely fond of lawns. It is unlikely that you will be able to convince your folks to let you turn their prize lawn into a wildflower meadow any time soon. However, you might be able to convince them that a small patch of long grass, say about 1 yard square (1 m²), would be a great science experiment. Of course the bigger the better, but sometimes we have to start small.

DO NOT WALK ON GRASS

Why is grass so dangerous? BECAUSE it's full of blades!

variety is good for wildlife!

Wildlife love **trees and shrubs**. Think of a square of grass about the size of this book. Now think how many creatures you would be able to spot in that small space, it wouldn't be very many. Now think of a small bushy tree planted in that spot, reaching up with its many branches, twigs and leaves. How much wildlife would be able to live in your tree? It would be a lot more, an incredible increase in beasties using your garden, and all in the same amount of space.

Adding some **water** to your garden will work in the same way as adding trees or bushes. A tiny pond will quickly become home to insect larva and will be a great place for birds to drop in for a drink, but a larger pond will very soon become a drinking and bathing spot for a whole host of local wildlife and a breeding place for invertebrates and amphibians.

Old and **rotting wood** is an invitation for all kinds of slithering, creeping and crawling insects to set up home in a corner of your garden. And when they have arrived, all the animals that eat them will come calling.

WHAT IS BAD FOR WILDLIFE?

POLLUTION, TIN CANS AND ALL THAT TRASH!

Sadly animals are killed or injured by pollution all the time. Not just from the pollution of big factories and the actions of unthinking adults, but by the things that we all do, all the time. Tin cans, especially those with the lids still attached, plastic bottles, yogurt pots, plastic sandwich bags and shopping bags, glass, discarded netting and the plastic collars that hold cans together all cause animals to suffer.

Always remove the lids of tin cans and crush them before sending them to be recycled. Cut up plastic collars so no loops can get caught around the necks of hedgehogs or foxes. Try to do without the packaging that causes the problems in the first place!

SLUG PELLETS AND OTHER POISONS

There are lots of ways to garden for wildlife and keep your garden looking beautiful at the same time. The chemicals that are used to kill pests, like aphids and slugs, are able to do their job because they are poisonous. And while a frog won't eat a slug pellet, he will eat the slug who has just eaten the slug pellet. That slug will be poisonous and will kill the frog. The same goes for the small birds who eat large numbers of insects that have been poisoned by insect spray; the birds of prey that hunt the smaller birds will be poisoned too.

There is another way of controlling the unwanted effects of too many pests, start a partnership with the other creatures in your garden. Birds who eat the mini-beasts in the garden often also eat seeds and berries. If you can encourage these birds in by offering food and places to shelter, they will always be around to clean up the pests for you.

If you have special plants that some beastie finds simply irresistible you can help your army of good-guys by planting in clever ways and using other plants to help you, see pages 31 to 33 for hints on pest control and companion planting.

BONFIRES

To us autumn bonfires are a great treat, especially if we get to toast some marshmallows with friends and sip hot chocolate around the blazing fire. To animals, the big pile of logs, twigs and rubbish is a wonderful winter home, a perfect place to crawl inside to hibernate, until the evening when it is set alight! Keep your wildlife safe from harm by building the woodpile on the day of the bonfire so that no curious creature has time to investigate and settle down inside for their winter sleep.

A very tidy garden with lots and lots of very short grass with no other planting isn't a great habitat for either plants or animals. Lawns don't usually get long enough to let flower spikes shoot up. So, no flowers equals no visiting bees or butterflies. Simple.

Too much digging destroys the comfortable habitat that earthworms, beetles and other ground dwelling beasties enjoy. A little bit of digging is fun and is needed in order to plant a desirable plant or to weed out an invader. But digging all the time isn't helpful to your garden guests.

What gets bigger the more you take away?

^ hole!

PLANTS AND PLANTING

Plants are the beginning of life and they are the beginning of the wonderful world that exists in your garden.

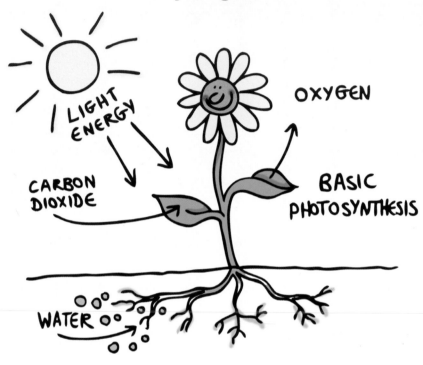

LIGHT ENERGY

OXYGEN

CARBON DIOXIDE

BASIC PHOTOSYNTHESIS

WATER

Plants combine water from the soil with the carbon dioxide from the air and change it into sugar in their leaves. They use the energy from sunlight together with the green pigment (colour) in their leaves to power the change. Then, they use the sugars to grow. The gas, carbon dioxide, is absorbed through their leaves and a waste gas, oxygen, is expelled from their leaves, luckily for us!

All plants need a certain combination of soil, water and sunlight in order to thrive. You can quickly and easily create a fantastic wildlife garden from almost nothing. A bit of ground or even a few pots of soil and you're on your way; wildflowers, vegetable plants and trees can all be grown from seed.

If you begin early in the year you will need to start your seeds off inside, where they are protected from the weather. Windowsills, porches and greenhouses are all perfect places to raise seeds.

250 years ago the scientist Joseph Priestly discovered photosynthesis when he conducted a series of experiments by putting a mouse in an air-tight jar. After a little while the poor little mouse collapsed and didn't revive until the jar was opened to let in fresh air. Then Priestly changed the experiment and put a potted plant in with the mouse and sealed the jar again. This time he found that the mouse was able to live and breathe normally and he concluded that the plant produced the oxygen that the mouse needed to survive.

why garden without peat?

Answer at the back of the book

TO PLANT YOUR SEEDS

You will need:

- **Pots or trays**
- **Small plastic bag**
- **Soil**
- **Pen and lollipop sticks and seeds.**

1. Prepare your pots or seed trays; use old yogurt pots, kitchen-paper tubes or discarded egg boxes, it really doesn't matter as long as you are able to make drainage holes in the bottom so your seeds aren't waterlogged. Remember that too much water will kill a plant as easily as too little water.

2. Fill the pot with peat-free potting soil or compost. Make sure that it is fine and free of lumps, as some of your seeds will be tiny and they won't be able to fight their way above the boulders in their pots!

3. Tiny seeds need to be sprinkled on the surface and covered with just the finest dusting of soil. Medium sized seeds need to be pushed ¼ of an in (0.6 cm) into the soil; larger seeds about ½ an in (1.3 cm), and really large seeds like nuts and acorns need to be at least an in below the surface.

4. Label each pot with the name and date of planting and water it gently. Cover pots containing small seeds with a plastic bag held above the soil by a popsicle stick, and place them in a warm spot. Once the seedlings germinate and emerge from the soil remove their cover and put them in a bright spot out of direct sunlight. Keep your plants moist, but not wet, and feed them once a week with home-made plant food. (see page 31)

5. When all risk of frost has passed, take your seedlings out to their new planting spot. Dig a hole about twice the width and depth of the pot so that the plant has an easy time sending its roots out into the soil, rather than trying to struggle through hard-packed earth. Gently knock the plant out of its pot and settle it into the hole, making sure the soil is at the same level on the stem as it was before. Back fill the hole and firm the soil around the roots.

If you are planting into a lawn or meadow area, give your plants a head start by clearing a space around them and keep them watered until they settle in and start growing strongly.

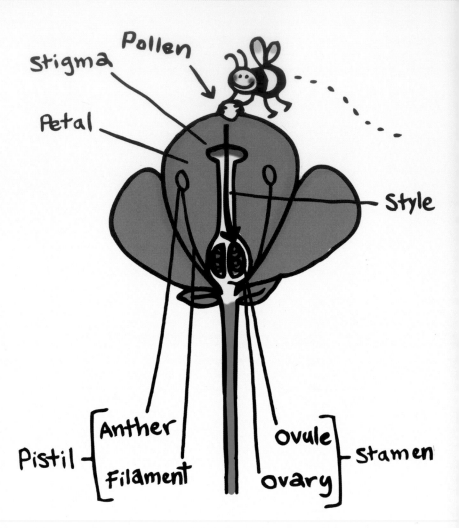

POLLINATION

Flowering plants are able to make seeds only when the male pollen lands on the female stamen. Some plants can manage to do this all by themselves with only the help of the wind. But very many plants need insects to help, so the plant uses brightly coloured petals, appealing scents and a sugary syrup called "nectar" to entice the insect in. While the insect is enjoying the sugary nectar, it accidentally picks up some pollen on its body. When the insect leaves to visit another plant in search of more treats, it will carry this load of pollen with it and accidentally deposit some onto the next plant. That is how pollination happens.

GERMINATION

A seed is a perfect time capsule that can often survive great extremes of heat and cold. Some seeds have been found that are still able to grow into plants even after 2,000 years! When the time and the conditions are right that little capsule will split open and begin to grow; given the right temperature and water the seed will turn into a plant. That is the miracle of germination.

SEED DISPERSAL

Some plants drop their seeds right in their own shadow, but if all seeds were to fall and germinate right at the feet of their parent, the space would soon get too crowded for anything to grow and the plants would soon die from lack of sunlight, water and nutrients. It's amazing that the plant kingdom has developed so many different ways to spread seeds about. Some plants set their seeds free to float away on the wind and some wrap their seeds in a prickly or sticky coat that will catch hold of passing animals. Many plants package their seeds in a tasty parcel that will entice animals to eat them, later to be deposited in a plop of droppings far away in new ground. Others develop wonderful exploding capsules that suddenly pop, throwing their seeds far and wide, while others even make the seed coats waterproof so that they can float away across whole oceans to find new ground to colonize.

TOOLS AND THE NITTY-GRITTY OF GARDENING

I'm ready!

What tools you need will depend on the size of your garden.

HOW TO BE AN AMATEUR NATURALIST

EQUIPMENT

To be a wildlife collector you first need to equip yourself with the kit that will let you study the creatures in your garden. It's possible to collect a huge and fascinating array of wildlife specimens, from feathers and pressed flowers to the empty shells of the numerous snails that you will find in your garden. Butterflies can be gently caught in a soft net to enable you to study them more closely and frogspawn can be scooped from your pond to be grown indoors so that you can watch them grow into frogs.

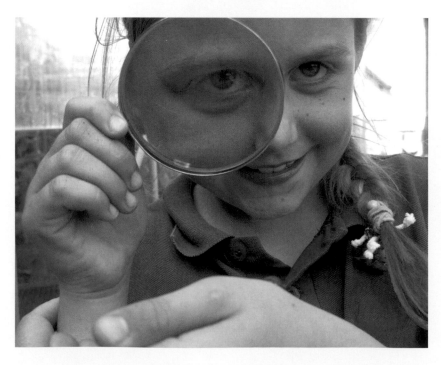

A magnifying glass is essential—the stronger the better. You can get really big magnifying glasses or tiny pocket lenses, or you can even make your own by filling a clear plastic bottle to the very top with water. Dry the outside of the bottle, turn it on its side and peer through, it is the curve of the bottle that provides the magnification.

You will need something to hold your specimens without damaging them, something to snip and cut with, a pooter (see the project opposite), a notebook and pencil. Masking tape and a permanent marker are perfect for labelling plant specimens. Match boxes, jars and old envelopes are all ideal for stashing your samples until you get them back to your nature table. A good field guide for identifying plants, birds or invertebrates is always handy, and binoculars and a camera are used to observe and record your sightings. All this stuff needs to be carried in something to keep it safe and on hand.

HOW TO MAKE A POOTER

You will need:

- **A jar with a plastic lid**

- **An 18 in (46 cm length of plastic hose (available from hardware and DIY shops)**

- **A small piece of very fine netting—old tights are perfect**

- **An elastic band.**

A pooter is a device that we use to pick up small insects without harming them. Sucked up through a small pipe, your specimen plops gently into the jar where you can observe it without any unnecessary handling. Netting on the end of the pipe that you suck through prevents insects becoming your afternoon snack!

1. First you need to make two holes in the lid of the jar. These holes need to be the exact size of the hose; any larger and the air will escape around the edges of the pipe and your pooter won't work properly. Make the holes with an adults help by heating a metal skewer over a candle flame. When the skewer is hot use it to melt two holes in the lid.

2. Cut the hose in two and push each length through the holes in the lid, plug any gaps with cotton wool or tape.

3. Cover one of the pieces of hose with netting on the end that will be inside the jar. Hold it in place with the elastic band. Now screw the lid on the jar, adjust the hose to the right length and try it out. Remember to suck through the hose that is covered by netting!

What do you get if you cross an insect with a rabbit?

Bugs bunny!

WATCHING WILDLIFE IN THE FIELD

You don't need a field to "watch wildlife in the field"; it's just a scientist's way of saying that you are observing your creatures in their natural habitats rather than in a laboratory.

Taking notes and keeping a nature diary

Some people like taking loads of notes when they are out and about, but others don't like it so much. If you are observing something in the garden that you won't be able to study later it may be a good idea to jot down everything you notice about it in a nature diary. Your nature diary can also include things like drawings, where you were when you spotted it and even the time of day. This is especially fun to do if it's something very unusual; maybe a fox visiting your garden or a sparrow-hawk taking its chance at your bird table.

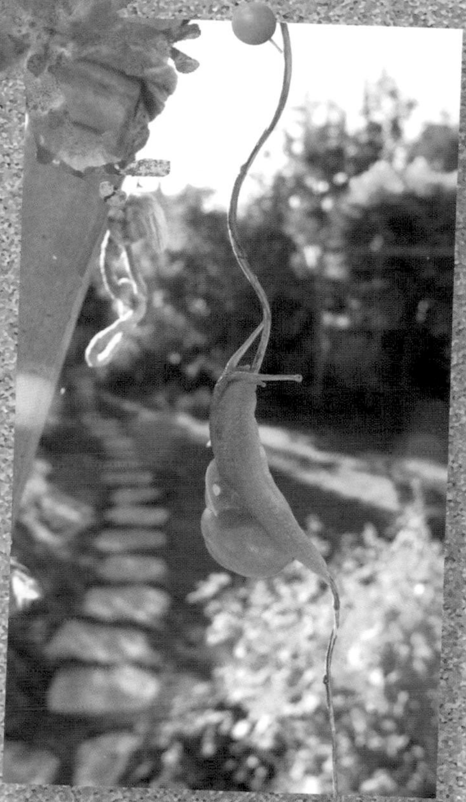

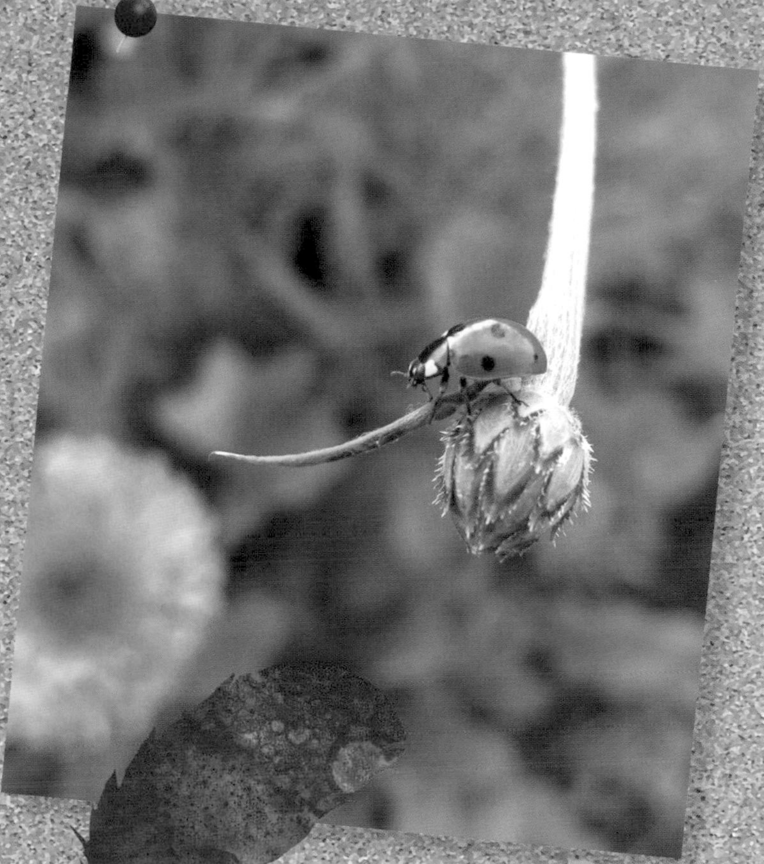

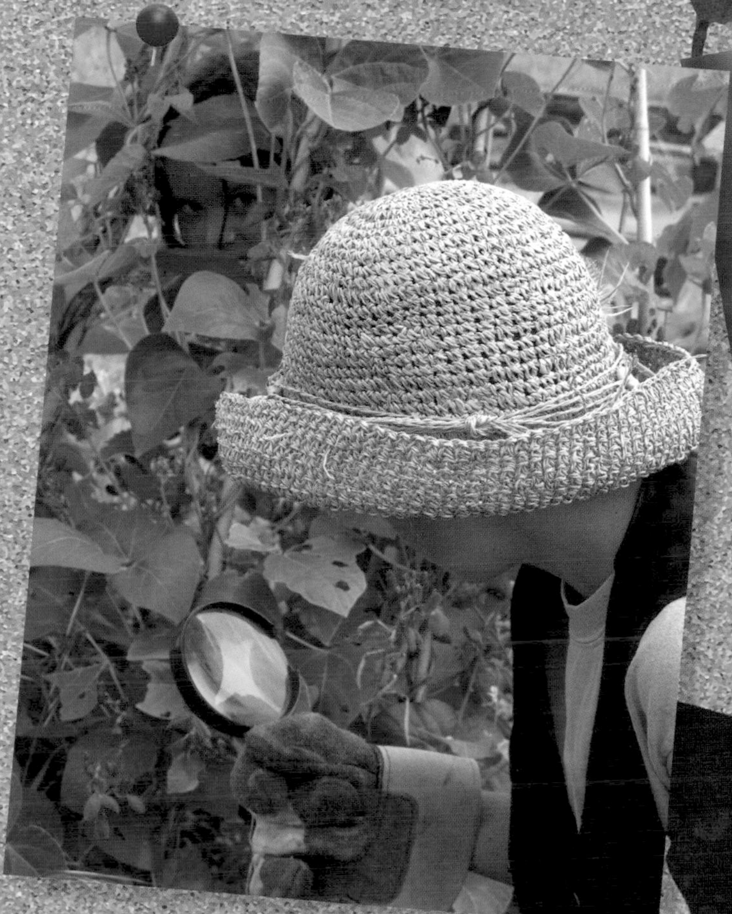

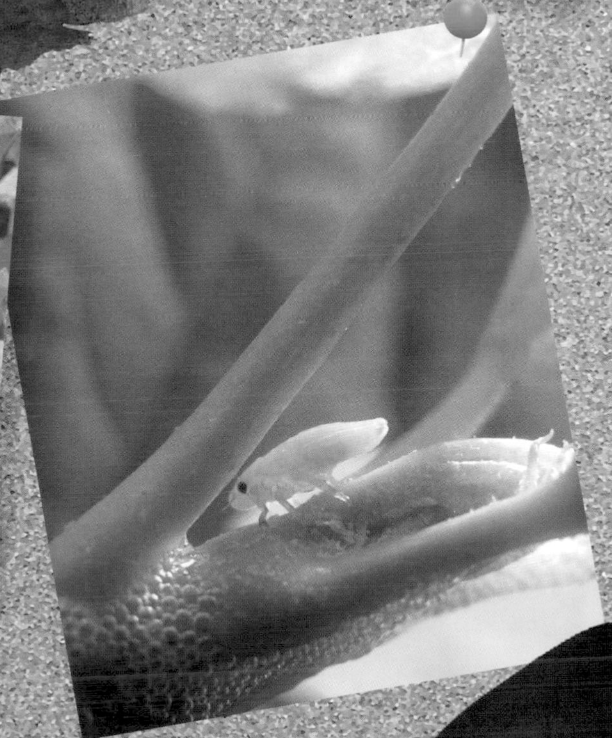

Taking photos of the wildlife in your garden is fun, especially when you look back at it after a few weeks. Try making a time-lapse sequence of something in your garden and making a flip book; a flower growing and changing into a seed head; a spring-time tree bursting into buds and leaves; even a clump of frogspawn developing into tadpoles. How cool is that!

If you have a tape recorder, or a mobile phone, or a video camera, you can begin to record the **sounds of your garden**. Birds are not the only things that make recordable sounds, squirrels chattering and scolding in a tree, even the sound of a wasp chewing up wood on a hot day can make a fascinating recording.

HOW TO MAKE SOUND RECORDINGS

The dawn chorus is the ideal time to sneak out and switch on the recorder, not only because birds are at their most vocal at this time, but also because there are fewer of the other sounds around which might spoil your recording. Everyone else will be in bed!

If you are a city gardener, or you live beside a busy road, you may find an umbrella is a very useful tool to help get clear and uninterrupted sound recordings. Sit with the noise pollution behind you and open the umbrella, resting the handle on your shoulder. Point your sound recorder in the direction of your subject. The umbrella will do two things, it will shield unwanted noises and it will concentrate the bird song or squirrel chatter by bouncing the sound waves back towards the microphone. There are many books and CDs that will help you identify the birdsong and sounds that you might hear.

Binoculars are a must but they can be tricky and frustrating to begin with. Start off by focusing on familiar objects around your garden as you learn to use them. Often, smaller binoculars are more useful in gardens as the large professional ones are just too powerful and they won't let you focus on closer objects, like the bird table on your lawn. Be careful to handle your binoculars with care as a heavy jolt can dislodge the lenses inside and make them useless.

Wildlife tends to be quite shy so to be able to watch certain creatures you need to be hidden. Naturalists, bird watchers and wildlife cameramen are all able to do their job because they make a **hide** in which to sit and wait and watch. Some hides can be very fancy, but a simple dark sheet hung over some sticks will do the trick. More important than how it looks is how it sounds. Most wildlife will soon get used to a new feature in the garden, like a small play tent, or a homemade hide, but if it is made of noisy material, the creatures you are trying to watch will constantly be startled away.

When you are inside your hide you may need food and drink to keep you going. Leave the packets, crunchy food and slurpy straws for another time or you may find you scare your subjects away when you tuck into your snack!

TO MAKE A HIDE

You will need:

- **A large sheet or piece of dark fabric**

- **Sturdy sticks or bamboo canes about 6 ft (1.8 m) long**

- **String or garden twine.**

1. Beg or borrow a piece of dark colored fabric (old sheets or curtains are perfect) and root out five sturdy sticks or bamboo canes.

2. Choose the best spot for your hide. Is there plenty of potential activity in the area? Can you get to your hide easily without attracting too much attention? Is the spot going to be comfortable enough for you to sit in for long periods? Push the sticks into the ground to make a circle about 4 ft (1.2 m) across and carefully bend the sticks together to make a tepee. Tie the top of the sticks together securely.

3. Now decide in which direction you will be doing most of your watching and place the doorway on the opposite side so you can sneak in without disturbing your wildlife. Drape the fabric around the poles and, using your string, tie it at the top where the sticks meet and peg it down around the edges so the wind doesn't blow it around and startle your subjects.

4. Settle yourself inside your hide in a comfortable position to check out the correct height for your viewing slits. Carefully make several slits in the fabric with some scissors; make sure the slits are only just big enough for you to peer out and poke your binoculars and camera through. At this point you can add all sorts of camouflage; lean some branches against the hide and push leaves around the base to stop it looking too man-made. When you are satisfied with your work, go away and leave it for a day or two to allow the garden creatures and regular visitors to get used to this new addition to their space. Once you notice that the birds are returning to the area, you can begin to use the hide.

If you are sharing your hide with a friend, it's a good idea to have some signals sorted out so you can communicate without talking. And if you do talk, don't whisper—talking very quietly is better than whispering because the sound waves don't travel so far!

SQUARE METER GARDEN

Mark off a square yard (1 m) of your garden. Hammer some pegs firmly into the ground at each corner and tie some string around each peg. Now, for ten minutes each day get down on the ground and observe the comings and goings in your square yard garden. It wont be too long before you begin to recognize some of the creatures in your patch—what are they doing, what are they eating? You can carefully mark some of the creatures in the area to see how far they stray or if they stay put. Keep a record of the everyday goings-on. It is a fascinating mini-world that you will soon begin to understand minutely.

SNAIL TRAILS

Study how far your garden snails roam by marking their shells with a small dot of nail polish (snail polish?) or correction fluid. Choose different colors for different parts of the garden to see if one group of snails travels more than others. Find out if snails will return to their own patch by collecting a group from one part of your garden and setting them down in another part. Don't forget to keep a record!

where do you find giant snails?

on the ends of giants fingers!

NATURE LAB. COLLECTING AND STUDYING WILDLIFE

Once you have begun to gather specimens. It is very satisfying to be able to start building up collections of all the different artifacts and creatures that you have found.

Flowers and leaves can be kept forever if they are pressed flat and dried. The Natural History Museums in London, and in New York, still have thousands of plant specimens that were collected by the explorers who first discovered Australia and the Americas.

A flower press is easy to improvise by using the pages of an old book. Telephone directories are ideal for pressing flowers and leaves because the soft paper absorbs moisture from the plant. Place your leaves and flowers flat between the pages without overlapping, carefully close the book and then stack more books on top. The heavier the weight pressing down on the leaves and flowers, the flatter and better preserved your specimen will be. Check on your specimens after a couple of weeks. Once they are completely dry, you can keep your plant specimens safe by sandwiching them between the pages of a photograph album, or use them to illustrate and decorate your nature diary.

Small items, such as snail shells, small animal bones, seed heads and foundling eggs can be stored in plastic food trays or wooden boxes.

There are many types of creepy crawlies in your garden. **Arthropods** are creatures that don't have an inner skeleton like we do. Instead they have a hard outer casing to protect themselves, like the hard 'skin' of beetles and spiders, or the shell of a snail.

Scientists use special words to identify groups of arthropods, "insect" is a name given to any arthropod that has three body segments and six legs. Be careful though; some insects aren't always easy to identify like this. For example a caterpillar is an insect, but it can look as if it has many legs and only one long soft body part, but look at the adult butterfly, and you can quickly see that it is indeed an insect.

Bug hunting: when is a bug not a bug? When it's a beetle, a caterpillar, an ant or a spider. A bug is a particular type of arthropod that has sucking mouthparts. In other words it doesn't bite or chew, it pierces and sucks! But the word bug is often used to describe any type of creepy-crawly. Even some entomologists call themselves bug hunters.

BUTTERFLY OR MOTH?

What makes a moth a moth, or a butterfly a butterfly? Look at the wings and the antenna. The wings of a moth are usually laid flat over its body when at rest, while a butterfly usually holds its wings together, pointing upwards. Most moths have feathery antennae while butterflies have club shaped antennae. Moths are often covered with a thick coat of hair. Although there are exceptions, moths tend to rest during the day and only becoming active when the sun goes down while butterflies are most active in the daylight.

In the olden days bell jars were used by naturalists and scientists to protect specimens in their laboratories. The jars were placed over their delicate specimens to keep them free from dust and damage. Proper bell jars are difficult to find, but large jars can be upturned over a fine specimen and will do the job just as well.

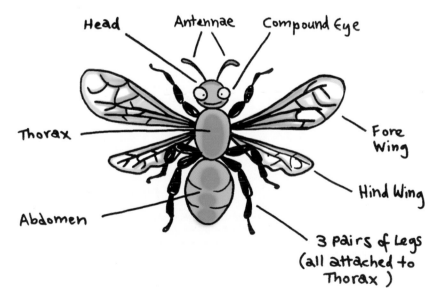

Head
Antennae
Compound Eye
Thorax
Abdomen
Fore Wing
Hind Wing
3 pairs of Legs
(all attached to
Thorax)

MOUNTING FOUNDLING INSECTS

Very thin pins are used for displaying the dead insects you will discover on your forays around your garden. Push the pin through the thorax (body) of the insect while supporting it carefully and then push the pin into a piece of cardboard. Use a good field guide (guide book) to identify your specimens. If your writing is very neat and small you can write your labels by hand. If this is very tricky, try typing it into a computer and then changing the font size until it is very small, but still readable.

Microscopes are a fantastic window onto a fascinating micro-world. There is really no other way to really appreciate the scales on a moth's wing, the teeming life in a drop of water or the lenses of a fly's eye.

Begin by studying everyday things like your own hair or a dragonfly wing. Remember to use the sun or a lamp to cast the light through your specimen. Doing drawings is a great way to record what you can see through the lens. You don't need a very expensive or complicated microscope; any microscope will open up a whole new world.

How many eyes does a fly have? Can you count them?

Answer at the back of the book.

The first microscope was invented by a Dutch spectacle maker around 1600. He found that by putting two lenses together he could make tiny things appear much larger. But even cleverer than that, another Dutch inventor found that it was the exact curve of the polished glass that was responsible for the magnification, and he invented a tiny lens that could make things look 270 times bigger! For the first time people found that there was life as small as bacteria that couldn't be seen with the naked eye!

TERRARIUMS AND AQUARIUMS

You can keep all sorts of animals in terrariums and aquariums in your nature lab. Frog and toadspawn are fascinating to watch as they grow. Look on page 60 for step-by-step instructions. Beetles like the rove beetles and ground beetles that you find in your compost heap are easy to keep in small containers inside, or you can watch the lifecycle of mealworms by growing them indoors.

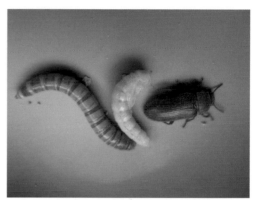

TO MAKE A MEALWORM COLONY

You will need:

- A large see-through tub or a small aquarium with a lid

- Some bran, (a ground-up grain similar to flour—available from supermarkets)

- A few live mealworms (available from pet shops and bird food suppliers).

1. To begin, make sure your tub is clean and dry. Poke a few very small holes in the lid to provide ventilation. Place a 2 in (5 cm) layer of bran in the bottom of the container—this will be both their food and their habitat—and gently place your mealworms in their new home. Keep your beetle farm in a warm spot out of direct sunlight, don't let them get too hot or too cold.

2. Add more bran to your farm when it is needed and keep watching. Your mealworms will grow longer and plumper until they are about ¼ of an in (0.6 cm) long when they will begin to transform into the next stage of their lifecycle, the pupa. This is the stage when they change from

worm-like creatures into proper beetles. As the beetles emerge from the pupal case, they will be pale and quite soft. Over the next few hours their exoskeletons will harden in the air and darken to their adult colouring. The adult beetles rarely fly preferring to scurry around on the surface of the soil where they will feed on bran and small pieces of vegetables or fruit.

3. Top the bran with a few pieces of bark or small pieces of rotting wood. Clean out any pieces of vegetable matter before it begins to rot. When you have completed your observations you can release your pets back into the compost heap.

HABITATS

FLOWERS AND VEGGIES IN THE WILD GARDEN

The veggie or flower garden is a wonderful habitat for all sorts of garden wildlife. Birds can find nectar, fruit, seeds and nesting material here, as well as a smorgasbord of creepy-crawlies to feast upon. Insects and spiders, to say nothing of slugs and snails, are right at home in your garden.

The key to a happy plot is **balance**, the right numbers of each type of plant and animals, and the right way to control them. The wildlife garden begins with the plants and it keeps on going with the right management, think of your garden as a zoo, rather than a garden.

Your garden animals, be they spiders, sparrows or snakes, need somewhere to hide, somewhere to rest in the sun, and shelter from the weather, and something tasty to eat.

TEN GOLDEN RULES

1. Don't tidy up too quickly. Unless there are diseased plants, leave some of the old stalks and fading plants where they are to provide a home for insects, seeds for birds and camouflage for reptiles and mammals.

2. Plant flowers in among your veggies and visa versa, this will attract bees, butterflies and other pollinating insects to your veggie plants so they will pollinate them as well. Some plants, like runner beans, need their flowers to be pollinated by visiting insects or they won't be able to make beans.

3. Don't use chemicals to get rid of the beasties that you don't want! Use other ways, like barriers (putting something in the way to stop pests munching on your precious plants), traps, or picking pests by hand. And avoid the chemicals that are used for feeding plants too, by making your own fertilizer. Fill a large bottle or bucket with nettles or comfrey leaves and cover with water. Forget about it for a couple of weeks then use it diluted at a rate of one part soup to nine parts water, be careful though: it's smelly!

4. Have some water in your garden. A bird bath will invite birds in and they will stay around to feast on aphids, blackflies and other fruit and flower pests. A mini-pond or even just a big bowl or a bucket, will encourage frogs, dragonflies and small mammals into your plot. Don't forget to put some stones in the water so any animal or bird has a safe place to perch while drinking and a step to clamber on if they fall in.

5. Beautiful bull finches are rather fond of your precious tree blossoms, and as we know that fruit can only grow from a fertilized flower it would be a terrible shame if your visiting birdlife stripped a tree of flower buds before they have a chance to open. This is easily avoided though, by putting a net over a small tree or by hanging twirling, flashing CDs from the branches to scare the birds away until the flowers have opened. Leave the CDs in place if you have a cherry tree or fruit bushes, especially currents!

6. Leave some loosely dug bare earth in a sunny corner in the garden for bees to burrow into and for solitary wasps to collect earth to line their nests.

7. Mulch is a layer of any material that stops water evaporating and stops weeds from growing. Mulch the area between your flowers and veggies, That way earth-dwelling beetles and bugs have somewhere dark and damp to roam and at the same time you reduce the amount of watering you may need to do in the hotter periods. On top of that, you are easily able to walk between your plants and you won't need to weed!

8. Grow plants especially for wildlife—teasles, sunflowers, herbs, calendula and marigolds, lavender, marjoram and other herbs. These will encourage the birds and insects to visit that will help to control your uninvited guests.

9. Mix it up! Include water, fruit trees and bushes, feeding stations, log piles, climbers, and animal shelters.

10. Enjoy your garden and have fun!

Do you know that not all slugs are a gardeners' enemy? Many slugs feed on rotting vegetation like fallen leaves and old fruit, and others are carnivores who eat garden pests like other slugs, beetle grubs and snails

Try using old cardboard boxes, old carpet, planks of wood, plastic, wood chippings, thick layers of grass clippings or anything else that will save water and keep weeds from growing.

How do you stop rabbits digging up your garden?

Hide the shovel!

Rabbits and Mice are great on the lawn, in the woods and scurrying around in the long grass, but in the veggie garden they aren't quite so cute. Entice the mice into another part of your garden by leaving out seed treats for them to enjoy, as a mouse in the veggie plot can remove every one of your carefully planted peas almost as quickly as you can plant them! Rabbits on the other hand will only be deterred by a very sturdy fence or wire cage and some very careful observations. If there is a way in, they will find it, just think of Peter Rabbit.

Create extra hidey holes and habitats by including lots of interesting houses for various species, just imagine what you can include!

WILDLIFE FRIENDLY PEST PATROL

Flying insects like carrot flies and cabbage white butterflies can be stopped from laying eggs on your plants simply by draping a fine net over the row. Add some strong smelling plants like chives and onions to help disguise the scent of your vegetables.

Tubes made from plastic bottles or kitchen rolls slid over your seedlings will stop grubs from feasting on your tender plants.

Trap slugs by laying squares of damp cardboard or planks of wood in between your plants; the slugs will cosy down in the dark and damp, just waiting for you to pick them up and dispose of them.

Wipe off colonies of aphids and blackflies with a gloved hand or spray them off with water from an old washing up bottle.

Caterpillars and other large pests can be picked off by hand whenever they become a problem.

In Britain during the Second World War food was scarce and rationing was introduced. People were ordered to dig up their flowers and to plant fruit and vegetables instead. Children were used to help feed the country by looking after school vegetable gardens and by going on butterfly patrol. Some lessons were spent catching large white butterflies to stop them laying eggs on the cabbages in the gardens.

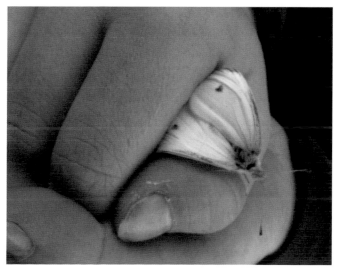

Slurp!

Pigeons are frequent visitors to flower and vegetable gardens were they have a habit of pulling up small plants. You can deter them by laying a net curtain or some twiggy sticks over your seedlings until they are big enough to escape their attentions. If you have put a watering hole in your garden watch the next time a pigeon pays a visit,they don't scoop water up like other birds when they drink, they suck it up instead.

What job did pigeons have during the Second world war?

Answer at the back of the book.

WHEN IS A WEED NOT A WEED?

Is a dandelion a weed? How about a stinging nettle? It all depends on who is looking at it and where it is growing; young dandelion leaves are delicious in salads and in some countries they are sold in food markets. The roots have been used for years to make soft drinks and dandelion coffee. Nettles can be used to make a really nice soup, and any passing painted lady or peacock butterfly will tell you that nettles are her caterpillars' favourite food.

Water is precious and because there are more people than ever before, and because most of us live with things like washing machines and showers and other day-to-day water-consuming gadgets, we are using up the available water at a faster and faster rate. We can save water in our gardens by mulching, by lining all pots in the garden with plastic to slow evaporation, by using a watering can instead of a garden hose and by making really good use of gutters and water butts so we use the water from the clouds instead of the tap!

LIFE IN A COMPOST HEAP

All gardens should have a compost heap. It will turn kitchen scraps into lovely rich earth and you need to do almost nothing to make it happen! A compost heap is at the very heart of wildlife gardening. It is a unique habitat and it has its own lifecycle. All sorts of creatures call the compost heap their home, from earthworms, bugs and beetles to slow worms, hibernating lizards and breeding snakes.

To build a proper working compost heap you only need a small space, about 4 ft (1.2 m) square and preferably in a sunny spot, and a few basic ingredients. It's a bit like baking a cake, put in the right stuff, give it a stir, leave it in the warmth and hey, presto! Your heap is cooked and ready. And the great thing about owning a compost heap is that not only are you being eco-friendly because you are recycling all your kitchen and garden waste, and making your very own garden compost and fertilizer, you are also making one of the best wildlife habitats in the garden. You are terrific!

What makes it so difficult for a robin to pull a slippery earthworm out of the soil?

Answer at the back of the book.

LAYERED
COMPOST
HEAP

yum!

Build your heap up in six in (15 cm) layers; a layer of 'greens' and a layer of 'browns'. Every now and then throw in a spade of garden soil to add the mini-beasts and micro-organisms that keep the whole thing working. Keep it cooking by turning it over using a spade and spray it with water if it is dry.

GREENS

Keep a small compost bin by your kitchen sink to make collecting every suitable scrap easy and quick, it soon adds up.
- Fruit and vegetable scraps and peelings
- Pet bedding and waste from any vegetarian pet
- Grass clippings, weeds and garden vegetation
- Tea bags, coffee grounds
- Egg shells
- Nettles, comfrey and pea and bean roots
- Faded cut flowers
- Used kitchen paper towels.

BROWNS

To help your compost to rot quickly, tear or cut the browns into small pieces.
- Newspapers, scrunched up into balls
- Cardboard, shredded and torn
- Fallen leaves
- The needles and soft branches of your Christmas tree, cut up small.

NOT WANTED

- Cooked food
- Cat or dog waste or the litter from any meat-eating pet
- Any meat or fat
- Any diseased plant material.

If you stick to the plan you will have a whole pile of lovely crumbly garden compost to add to your beds and borders or to use to plant your seedlings in six months!

Make a perfect wild garden compost heap by building the sides up with some old pallets, or a wood frame. Build it straight onto the ground so that invertebrates and other beasts can easily colonize your heap.

WORMS

What can see but doesn't have eyes, what can hear but doesn't have ears and what can breath but doesn't have lungs? A worm—worms are able to detect light, even though they don't have eyes, they breath through their skin and they hear things through the vibrations that pass through their bodies.

Worms are **hermaphrodites**, which means that they are both male and female at the same time. After they have mated, both worms are able to lay eggs.

Contrary to what many people think, you won't get two worms if you cut one in half! Sometimes the head end of the worm, which contains the brain (and the worms' many pairs of hearts) will regenerate some segments and will be able to live, but the tail end will always die.

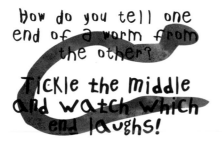

How do you tell one end of a worm from the other?

Tickle the middle and watch which end laughs!

How long is the longest earth worm in the world? As long as a ruler, as tall as a person or as long as a stretch limousine?

Answer at the back of the book

BEETLES

In colder climates many beetles and other invertebrates are not able to survive through the winter; some cope by burying very deep into the ground and others by laying their eggs or pupating in a warm corner during the colder months. Well-made compost heaps are perfect places for beetles and other invertebrates to overwinter as the decaying action of the plant material produces enough heat that the centre of the heap will remain above freezing, no matter what the weather outside.

Rove beetles and ground beetles are the most numerous beetles in the compost heap. They are predators and happily munch their way through the not quite so desirable beasties that we find in the garden and compost. You can observe the life-cycle of beetles like these by raising some mealworms in a terrarium indoors. See page 29 for tips and instructions.

One in every five animals on earth is a beetle, that is quite a number of beetles on our planet!

HUNDREDS AND THOUSANDS

Centipedes (which means hundred feet) are the hunters and millipedes (thousand feet) are the hunted! Centipedes are quick and agile and they hunt all sorts of mini-beasts including millipedes. Centipedes have poisonous fangs, but the venom in British centipedes is harmless to humans. Millipedes are slower and they only feed on rotting vegetation and not on other beasties.

You will find many different species of millipedes and centipedes in and around the lovely dark dampness of your compost pile and you may even find their nests. Some centipedes lay their eggs one at a time and then leave them to fend for themselves, while others will lay their eggs

in a comfortable hollow and stay with them, cleaning and caring for them, for up to a month. The type of centipedes that live in the soil are the push-me-pull-yous of the invertebrate world, able to travel backwards just as easily as forwards, while millipedes are the mini-skunks, as they have perfected the skill of expressing a poisonous spray when threatened!

Why did the millipede dropped from the football team? Because it took him too long to put his boots on!

EARWIGS

Earwigs got their name because it was believed that they would crawl into the ear of their sleeping victim and feast on their brain! Didn't people believe some curious things? Earwigs make very good mothers. While most insects give birth to eggs or young and tootle off and leave their babies to fend for themselves, earwig mums stand guard over their young for up to four weeks, until the cute little babies are able to look after themselves.

The scientific name for slow worms is anglis fragilis (as in fragile) and refers to their 'breakable' tail.

One wise slow-worm lived to be a very venerable 54 years old!

SLOW WORMS

Slow worms are actually legless lizards, so if you ever need to pick one up make sure you don't grab it by its tail, or, just like any other lizard, you may find yourself holding the tail while the rest of the animal makes a rather desperate bid for freedom. You can easily tell a slow worm from a snake. Slow worms are able to blink, unlike snakes, and upon close examination, the join between the body and the tail is quite easy to see.

Slow worms give birth to live young and they are most active at night. Some snakes give birth to live young but others lay eggs. The warmth of a compost heap is the perfect winter home or nest site. If you are really lucky you may find a slow worm curled up in your heap or a snake using the warmth to help hatch her eggs.

How many legs does a centipede really have? How about a millipede?

Answer at the back of the book.

LONG GRASS AND MINI-MEADOWS

Letting a patch of your lawn grow long will let the grasses and other plants develop flowers and seeds. That means butterflies and bees will visit to lay their eggs and feed on nectar. Spiders will move in and ants will build their nests. Crane flies will fly in to lay their eggs and birds will follow. With all the invertebrate activity in your mini-meadow, the mammals, reptiles and amphibians will soon move in.

The easiest and most reliable way to plant a flowering meadow is to plant plugs (small seedlings) in the lawn and then let the grass and your new plants grow up together. Quite often a wildflower meadow that is sown from seed ends up being a bit of a disappointment so to guarantee success start your seeds off indoors in a planting tray containing lots of little holes, that way you can nurse your seedlings until they get big enough to plant among the grasses and they will be more able to look after themselves.

The easiest way to tell the difference between these animals is to take a close look at their body segments, centipedes have only one pair of legs on each segment while millipedes usually have two.

You will find many different species of millipedes and centipedes in and around

the lovely dark dampness of your compost pile and you may even find their nests. Some centipedes lay their eggs one at a time and then leave them to fend for themselves, while others will lay their eggs in a comfortable hollow log or hole in the ground and stay with them, cleaning and caring for them, for up to a month. During the whole nesting time the mother centipede won't leave her young even to find food. Centipede childhoods are long, about three years, and they can live for a further two years as a mature adult.

The type of centipedes that live in the soil are the push-me-pull-yous of the invertebrate world, able to travel backwards just as easily as forwards, while millipedes are the mini-skunks, as they have perfected the skill of expressing a poisonous spray when threatened!

You can discover who the visitors are to your garden by laying a **pitfall trap**. Choose a large, deep jar and dig a hole just deep and wide enough for the jar to fit snugly inside. To shelter your quarry from the sun and rain, place four evenly sized stones around the hole and lay a large flat stone securely on top. Check the trap at least once a day and record the creatures that you find inside. It's likely that you will occasionally trap mini-beasts that are rivals, either because they are predator and prey or because they are territorial, and so will see each other as intruders. Carefully approach the trap and lift the cover stone away. Lift the jar clear of the soil and place a lid on top while you take it to a shady spot to study your subjects. Even better leave the jar in place and, if the beasties are small enough, remove them from the jar with your pooter.

If you are lucky enough to trap a small mammal you must first put on thick gloves, then cover the jar, before removing it from the soil. As you lift the jar free, cover it with a dark cloth, most animals will feel less threatened if they are kept in the dark. Carry your subjects to a safe place, and release them into your terrarium for studying. Keep the room dark and make sure you move slowly and gently so as not to startle your captive.

VROOM!

Some butterflies carefully lay their eggs a few at a time, well hidden on the undersides of leaves. Others fly over their chosen plants and drop their eggs like bombs in the hope that they will land in the right place.

Blue butterflies, like the rare Large Blue, have a wonderfully strange life-cycle. After mating the female butterfly lays her egg on a plant leaf. When the little egg hatches, the tiny caterpillar begins to eat and soon, plump and well fed, he drops to the ground where he is found by a certain type of red ant. This ant strokes the caterpillar's tummy which makes the caterpillar release a sweet liquid. This is just what the ant wants and she laps up this sweet 'milk' until, suddenly, the caterpillar gives a little start and curls up. Now, the ant doesn't want to lose her caterpillar cow, so she gently picks up her caterpillar and carries it back to her nest and tucks him up, safe and sound, in the ant nursery. All ants visit it to feed it and to give it a stroke and to take a drink. But our little caterpillar isn't a very good house guest, as, snuggled down in the ant burrow, it proceeds to devour its adopted

siblings, the real ant larvae. After a while the caterpillar spins itself a cosy cocoon and snuggles down to transform into an adult. Fully grown, it crawls to the mouth of the burrow and emerges into the daylight to spread its beautiful blue wings and fly away to find a mate.

You can make your own fascinating **butterfly house** to watch caterpillars grow and develop into cocoons and hatch out into beautiful butterflies and moths.

Always collect the eggs yourself so that you can be sure that, when you eventually release the adult back into the wild, it will be going back to its proper habitat. The best butterflies to observe are the most common, such as the peacock, the large (cabbage) white or the very common scarlet tiger moth.

TO MAKE A BUTTERFLY HOUSE

You will need:

- **A large water bottle with the top cut off**

- **A square of netting**

- **A large elastic band**

- **A jar with a lid**

- **Kitchen paper.**

1. Cut the netting so that it is about 2 in (5 cm) larger than the top of the water bottle. Lay a sheet of kitchen paper on the bottom of the bottle, to make clean-up easier.

2. Punch some holes in the lid of the jar to hold the caterpillar's food plants and place the jar, full of water, in the bottom of the bottle.

3. When the butterflies lay their eggs on the leaves of your garden plants, snip the stem that is holding the leaves and place it into the jar. The butterfly will have laid her eggs on the correct plant so once the eggs hatch, the tiny caterpillars will have their favourite food available immediately. Cover the bottle with the netting held in place with the elastic band. Caterpillars are eating machines, You will need to keep up with their enormous appetites by giving them fresh food regularly.

Try looking on cabbages or nasturtiums for the yellow eggs of the large white butterfly, on the undersides of nettle leaves for the eggs of peacock or on wild comfrey plants for the eggs of the scarlet tiger moth. This last one hatches from their eggs very early in the year.

Butterflies taste with their feet and smell with their wings.

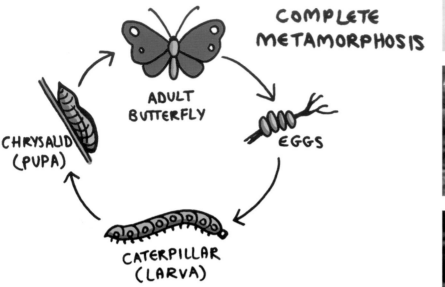

COMPLETE METAMORPHOSIS

ADULT BUTTERFLY

CHRYSALID (PUPA)

EGGS

CATERPILLAR (LARVA)

As it grows larger your caterpillar will go through several moults when it will stop eating and shed its skin. When it is ready to transform into a butterfly it will shed its skin for the last time, revealing the hard case of the chrysalis underneath. Inside this protective case the caterpillar makes the most astonishing alteration; his body parts change and move; some organs disappearing, some new ones being created. When, at last, this caterpillar potion has been magically transformed, the cocoon will begin to split open and a fully grown adult will emerge. First his wings will be crumpled and damp but soon they will dry out and your butterfly will be ready to fly. You can keep him for a day in the butterfly house, but soon it will be time to release him back into the wild of your garden where he can find nectar and a mate, and so the whole cycle can begin again.

Each time caterpillars molt it is called an "instar". Some caterpillars just get bigger each time but some take on a completely different form at each instar; so different that scientists were fooled into thinking they were completely different species.

To avoid being caught in spider webs many moths are able to shed the scales on their wings and escape.

You'll never get me up in one of those!

BEE AWARE

Many insects visit flowers to collect nectar and pollen but bumble bees have a special way of pollinating that other insects just cannot beat. Bumble bees are special because of the way they move their wing muscles. The super fast vibrations shake the pollen loose from the tiny holes in the anther of some plants, just like you shaking the salt out of a salt shaker. Without bumblebees plants like tomatoes and blueberries and many wildflowers couldn't be pollinated and couldn't make fruit. And that would be the end of them.

Provide plenty of bee homes around your garden by making bee posts, pots and bee hollows, the possibilities are endless. And don't forget to plant plenty of bee plants, the list is on page 90.

Bumble bees hatch their eggs just like chickens. In early spring a female bee will lay her eggs in a cosy hole, and then keep them warm and safe by sitting on them, just like a bird on a nest. To keep going until her eggs hatch she makes herself a little pot out of wax and fills it with honey that she makes from the nectar that she collects from the flowers in your garden. To keep her honey pot full she must visit hundreds of flowers each day, you can help by planting loads of nectar rich flowers for her to visit.

If you find a bumblebee stranded in the middle of a path it may have run out of energy. You could try giving it emergency rations in the form of sugar syrup. Mix up a teaspoon of ordinary sugar with two teaspoons of water until the sugar has dissolved and then pour it onto the path in front of the bee. The bee will detect it and may sip just enough to restore its energy and fly off in search of more nectar.

SPIDERS IN FIELDS AND MEADOWS

To kill a spider is thought to bring bad luck, while if you find a money spider (one of the really tiny spiders) and spin it gently three times around your head it is thought to bring you wealth.

In any square yard (meter) of grassy field it is estimated that you could count as many as 500 spiders!

Spiders occur in every type of habitat that you can create in your garden. In your mini-meadow, on flowers and grasses, and on patches of earth and warm stones you will be able to identify many different types, from the tiny crab spiders that can slowly change colour to match the flower they are sitting on, to the loving nursery web spider that builds a silk tent to protect her babies. Once you start to investigate you will see all sorts of different webs too. Hammock webs like horizontal slings are strung between twigs; orb webs come in all shapes and sizes, from perfectly round and neat to a ragged hexagonal; sheet webs draped over the surface of your

grasses, and many more. Perhaps the web that excites the most interest is that of the common garden spider when it is full of a clutch of tiny spiderlings.

Some spiders spin communal webs, though no one knows why. A Canadian farmer was astounded to find his whole 60 acre field was covered by a gigantic web populated by millions and millions of tiny spiders. Some scientists believe that because of the still, wet weather the tiny babies couldn't spin themselves their usual silken parachutes and drift away so they were all forced to spin their home webs in the same place. The web was so thick that it lasted for many weeks until the wind and weather finally destroyed it.

GRASSHOPPERS AND CRICKETS

It is considered very good luck to find a house cricket in your house, but if you hear it sing it means it will rain; but which part of its body is it using to make its song? Crickets use their wings to make their songs while grasshoppers use their legs. You can usually tell the difference between crickets and grasshoppers by taking a quick glance at the length of their antenna; as crickets tend to be more active at night, they need to use their long and slender antenna as feelers, while grasshoppers can cope perfectly with short and stumpy antenna. They hear the summer songs through ears on their legs or their bodies. Grasshoppers and crickets, like their cousins, the fleas, are terrific jumpers. While some species can fly during some stages of their lives, they usually rely on their powerful leg muscles to leap and jump around.

Crickets are ideal specimens to study in a terrarium; captured when they are tiny, they can be watched as they pass through their various moults until they reach adult size. Males can become argumentative at mating time, but if you are fortunate enough to capture both a male and a female you may be able to study the mating and egg laying process. Make sure you line the bottom of the terrarium with a thick layer of soil to provide a snug home for any eggs that are laid and regularly provide fresh food and moisture by giving them a regular supply of leafy twigs, lettuce, grass and fruit.

SHRUBS AND TREES

These are truly the high-rise buildings of the garden. Each level invites a different visitor; at the base, small mammals can nest, using the roots as the roofs of their burrows. A host of insects will live under the bark, and birds, spiders, moths and a myriad of other creepy crawlies will make their homes on the leaves and branches of the canopy.

As a wildlife gardener you can use and enjoy this wonderful habitat and even add to it and make it better by adding nest boxes for birds and insects and even small mammals. Try planting a climbing plant like honeysuckle at its base which will add nectar in the spring and summer and which will stop cats from climbing the trunk.

If you are lucky enough to have a tree within view of your window, that's terrific; but you don't need to wait years for a tree to grow before you can enjoy the fun. Even a small tree or a sapling will be able to support

feeders and nest boxes in a very short time, see the list of quick growing trees on page 90.

Begin adding to the tree by hanging feeders all over it. Use one of your feeders to hold nesting material instead of food, and don't forget the water! Make a **hanging bird bath** by suspending a shallow bowl from your tree from a braided holder, don't forget to place stones in the dish to give the birds somewhere to stand, and re-fill the dish with fresh water when the water level gets low.

Hang your bird feeder well away from cat hidey holes so nothing can creep up on your birds on silent paws!

MAKE A BIRD FEEDER OUT OF A PINE CONE

You will need:

- A pine cone (the bigger the better)

- A length of string or thin wire, some peanut butter (with no added sugar or salt)

- Some birdseed and a spoon.

1. Put the peanut butter somewhere where it will warm up, like an airing cupboard or a sunny window sill. This isn't essential, but it will make it much easier to work with.

2. Tie a 12 in (30 cm) piece of string or garden wire to the base of the pine cone and then push the peanut butter into all the crevices with the back of a spoon.

3. As a final delicious treat, roll the sticky cone in some birdseed. Hang it up outside where you can see the birds enjoying their dinner!

Woodpecker Goo is a lovely sticky, buggy stew that is perfect for woodpeckers and other bark feeding birds. Mix up some grated suet, dried mealworms and peanut butter in a bowl. Choose a log 3 to 4 in (8 to 10 cm) thick and about 10 in (25 cm) long. Drill a hole through the top to hold the wire and drill another eight or nine holes around the sides. Push your woodpecker goo into the holes and hang your feeder on a tree, close to the main trunk.

A log hanger is a quick, rustic feeder for birds that like to stand and feed. Hunt for a log that has one side that is flat or better yet, slightly hollow, a split log might do the trick! Attach some sturdy string to each end of the log and hang it onto a horizontal tree branch. Sprinkle bird seed, suet or mealworms on the flat surface and wait for your guests to appear.

Goldfinch are most often noticed in the autumn when they are feeding on seeds of thistles and teasels.

Wrens are tiny brown birds with really big voices. The male may build several nests for the female to choose from, but leaves each one unfinished. When the female has looked them over and made her choice, she adds the finishing touches by adding a cosy lining.

Blue tits are acrobatic and inquisitive and may well be the most common visitor to a bird table. Because they are so curious they are very satisfying visitors, as they will investigate any new feeding station with confidence. The old name for blue tits was "titmouse".

Blackbirds, like robins, take good advantage of garden activity and the warmth of cities and towns in winter. If you see a blackbird with its head cocked to one side as if it is listening for something, take a closer look, more probably it is looking out for worms and insect activity, its eyes don't swivel in their sockets as ours do, so it must turn its head in order to look around.

Sparrows are great fun to watch. A flock of sparrows feeding in a hedge is a busy sight and it's not unusual for a sparrow or two to join you at the picnic table as you enjoy your lunch outside. Groups of sparrows can become a nuisance as they bully other birds away from the bird table but this is easily dealt with by putting food out in different areas of your garden; they are so curious they will be quick to investigate a new feeding station. Unlike robins, sparrows are very sociable birds and they live happily in colonies, in towns, cities and the countryside. Their nests are messy constructions of twigs, feathers and dried stalks and they aren't fussy about where they build them either. Probably because they are so happy to invade our fields and gardens they have earned themselves a poor reputation. During the Second World War the British government even demanded that people destroy sparrows' nests wherever they were found so that the birds didn't eat the farmers' grain!

BLACKBIRDS ARE GOOD MIMICS AND CAN COPY THE SOUNDS OF THEIR NEIGHBOURHOOD SUCH AS RINGING PHONES AND EVEN SIRENS.

RAVEN

CARRION CROW

JAY

ROOK

MAGPIE

CHOUGH

JACKDAW

Corvids are the group of birds that include crows, rooks, ravens, jackdaws, magpies and jays. They are intelligent and curious and make very entertaining visitors to your garden.

A BOY GOES INTO A PET SHOP AND ASKS THE MAN FOR SOME BIRD SEED:

How many birds have you got?

None, I want to grow some!

BIRD BEAKS

Fruit + Bud Eater

Insect Hunter

Seed Cracker

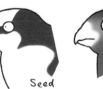
Meat Eater

A good field guide is a must for enjoying the birds who visit your garden. When you're observing your visitors pay close attention to their size, the shape of their beaks and the way they move, these are all excellent pointers to their identity.

If your garden is cat-free you can leave some nest boxes out in the autumn for birds to find the following spring.

Put out a selection of **bird boxes**, some with round holes and some with larger rectangular openings. Make sure the entrance hole is between 1 in (2.5 cm) and 1¾ in (4.5 cm) across and the height from the floor inside isn't so shallow that the tiny birds will fall out!

Make your box out of material which is waterproof and well insulated; metal or clay may get too hot in the sun and too cold at night (think of those tiny, naked baby birds!) and leave them untreated unless you are sure the paint is okay for wildlife.

TEAPOT NEST BOX: TUCK A TEAPOT DEEP IN A SHELTERED SPOT IN A HEDGE TO MAKE A LOVELY COSY HOME FOR BIRDS OR MICE.

Go seed collecting to gather the **seeds of native tree species**, especially those that flower and fruit. Better yet, allow a seedling to grow in your garden and grow an entire ecosystem! Many tree seeds are dropped by passing birds or buried by squirrels, and if these are allowed to grow where they sprout, they will send their roots down deep and wide and will often grow faster and stronger than a larger sapling that has been grown in a nursery in a pot. What could be nicer than having a tree that you have planted from a seed or that has been planted for you by one of your wild visitors?

You can sample the animal life that inhabits your tree by indulging in a **spot of tree bashing**. Check first that there are no birds' nests that might be disturbed by your activity. You may want to wear a hat and long sleeved shirt for this project. Have your collecting pots and envelopes ready, as well as your butterfly net, your pooter and a deep bucket.

Spread a light colored sheet beneath your tree or have some friends hold the corners of the sheet as high as they can. With a long stick rustle the leaves and branches of your chosen tree. When you have dislodged as many specimens as possible, gather the corners of the sheet together and gently shimmy the contents into one corner, then carefully and slowly empty everything into the bucket. You must work quickly and carefully now with your net, your pooter, and your hands, to collect the different specimens and place them in individual collecting pots. Don't forget to examine the leaves and twigs that fall as well, as they may have hitchhikers on board, like eggs or cocoons, or galls growing on leaves.

Examine the ground beneath your trees regularly for signs of the inhabitants high above. You may be lucky enough to find an owl pellet under a branch, or, if you have a hard surface beneath your tree, you will likely find the empty broken shells of snails. Thrushes have learnt to use paving stones and large rocks as anvils; a thrush will collect a snail and fly up to a roosting branch. There they will bash the snail on the branch to release it from its shell, or drop it on the rocks below to break the shell, and allow it to get at the tasty morsel inside. Ingenious!

Squirrels are frequent visitors to our gardens to some peoples delight and other peoples' annoyance. The grey squirrel is an alien invader who has made himself right at home, to the detriment of smaller red squirrels. However, if you can put up with him raiding your birdfeeders, grey squirrels can make wonderfully entertaining members of your garden community. Unlike most other creatures they aren't shy so they will continue their acrobatics even when you are quite close.

If squirrels are among your favorite garden guests, it may be fun to make a squirrel run out of a length of rope leading from their favorite tree to a feeding station. Try dangling nuts, seeds and fat balls in challenging places, then sit back and enjoy the squirrels daredevil antics!

PONDS AND BOGGY GROUND

A pond attracts all sorts of cool creatures, from frogs, toads and newts to dragonflies, water boatmen and pond snails. All these, in turn, attract other creatures, from bats to birds and even foxes. Even a large bowl of water will attract more wildlife than you can imagine, who will use it to drink from, to bathe in and to breed in. Some animals will spend their entire life-cycle under the surface while others will simply visit from time to time. Imagine the thrill of seeing a new creature in your garden and knowing the only reason it's there is because you gave it a perfect home. That really is wild!

You will need:

- A large plastic bucket or tub with no drainage holes

- Stones

- Water plants, especially oxygenating plants, and border plants—ask for 'hardy' plants that will survive through the winter

- Some plastic sheeting or a heavy-duty bin (garbage) bag

- A small fishing net or an old sieve to clean out your pond and to gently catch and examine your pond creatures, when they appear.

MAKE A MINI-POND

1. Use your spade to mark around the edge of your container so you know where to dig.

2. Dig out the hole and place the excavated earth onto the plastic sheet to make clean-up easier. Drop your tub into the hole.

3. Make a ladder with some of your stones to allow animals to climb out of the water easily. Even frogs and toads can find it difficult to scramble out of a smooth-sided pond.

4. Fill the pond with water from a water butt or rain barrel. Tap water will take several days to settle down and be fit for animals to live in.

5. Add your pond plants. Be sure to put them in at the correct depth, some plants like to be in several in/cm of water but some like to be very deep.

6. Plant perennials around two or three sides of your pond to make a nice hide-away for visiting creatures, and to provide patches of shade in your pond. Build a rockery on one side to make a hidey-hole for frogs and newts.

The first creatures to colonize your pond will probably be the larva of midges, gnats and mosquitoes, quickly followed by familiar members of the pond community; beetles and bugs, water snails, and the fascinating larva of mayflies, dragonflies and damselflies. Flatworms and leeches, as well as many other fascinating animals, will find their way into your pond on the feet of larger animals and birds, as well as hidden among the leaves of your new water plants.

Oxygenating plants are able to capture oxygen from the air and transfer it into the water—even water creatures need to breathe—they just do it in a different way to air breathing animals like us.

Top up your pond with fresh water if the level drops more than a couple of in.

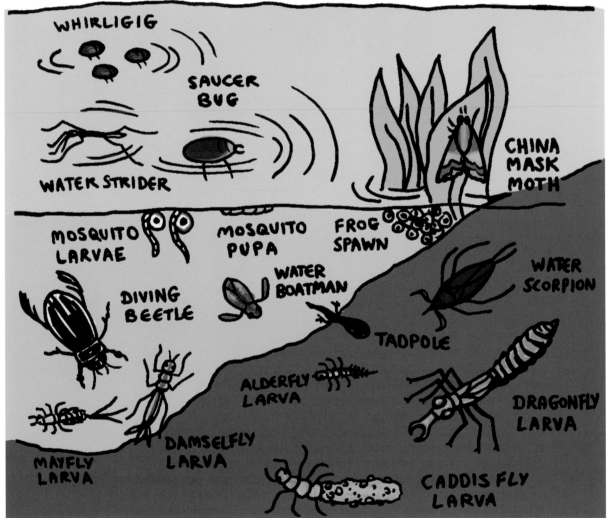

Toad hall. Provide a safe and sheltered home for your amphibians by making a toad hall close to the water, but safe from freezing temperatures and marauding invaders, like cats!

Begin by setting a plant pot on its side, and settling it into the soil so that it won't roll about. Cover the outside with dry leaves and grasses for plenty of insulation, and then surround it all around with small logs or large stones or bricks. Leave a frog-sized hole towards the front so that your guest can crawl inside, but don't make it so large that the weather can follow him in! Make sure everything is very stable so nothing can fall down or be knocked over. Your frog or toad will be happy and snug for many months over winter and may hide there to escape the heat of summer too.

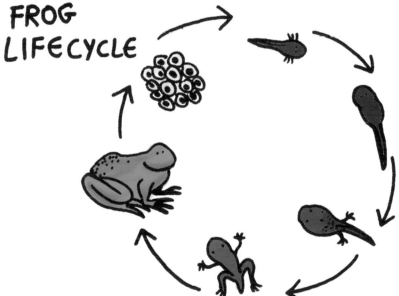

FROG LIFECYCLE

Can't tell your frog from your toad? It's easy...warty toads toddle and smooth frogs leap!

How does a frog feel when it has a broken leg? Very unhoppy!

HOW TO KEEP AN AQUARIUM OF FROGSPAWN

Choose a container that is watertight and a spot out of direct sun. If you can, fill your aquarium with tap water a week before you add your frogspawn, tap water contains chemicals that are harmful to pondlife so letting it sit for a week will allow the chemicals to disappear. If you need to supply a home to some frogspawn right away, allow the water to come to room temperature and add a water purifying tablet (meant for goldfish bowls) bought from a pet shop. It will clear the water for you and make it safe for your tadpoles.

Place some washed gravel in the bottom of the tank and sit some stones or rocks inside so that the tadpoles can clamber out of the water when they begin to develop legs. A few strands of **oxygenating** plants, available from pet shops and aquarium dealers (or better yet, your own or a neighbours pond) will keep the environment fresh and alive. Check it first, though, to make sure it isn't hiding any predators that will feast on your tadpoles or spawn.

Now add your frogspawn. As when you are introducing any creature to a new environment, you must do this gently to avoid shock. Float the sealed collecting bag in the your tank for an hour or two so that the water is the same temperature, then gently tip the eggs into their new home and sit back and wait. Don't forget to photograph them every few days to keep a record of their development. Once they have hatched you will need to begin feeding them. To begin with the tiny tadpoles are vegetarian and will nibble on the vegetation in the tank, as well as any morsels of rabbit or hamster food that you provide. Only add as much as they can finish, any leftovers will make the water dirty and will mean that you need to clean it out more often.

When the tadpoles begin to grow legs, their appetites change and they turn into carnivores! Give them fish flakes, available from pet shops (and the pet section of grocery stores) and if you have a pond or stream nearby, go daphnia fishing for the tiny flea-like creatures that swim about in fresh water. A few of these will keep your developing tadpoles busy and happy. Remember not to overfeed the tank.

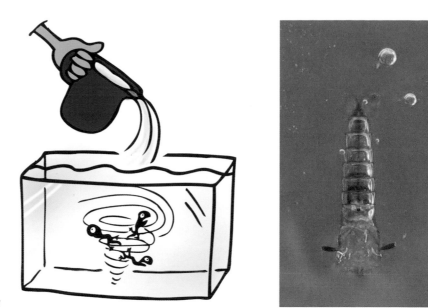

Once the front legs begin to appear, reduce the water level in the tank and start to introduce tiny live insects at meal times, your froglets are now learning to feed on grown-up food. Keep the insects small. Hunt around your garden, on roses and other flowers and on the tender stems and the undersides of leaves to find pests that can be harvested to feed your froglets. They will appreciate every mouthful!

Clean out your tank regularly by gently scooping out about half the water with a jug (kept especially for this purpose) and replacing it with fresh water that has been allowed to sit overnight. Pour the fresh water in very gently, slowing it down by pouring it over the back of a plate so you don't create a whirlpool effect!

Release your baby frogs back into the same pond from where you got them to limit the impact of your froggy observations on the environment. Tip them gently right at the edge of the water where they can hide among the vegetation, safe from predators.

YUM!

YUM!

YUM!

Two tadpoles were sitting in their tank: one said to the other, "I'll drive and you man the guns."

Sometimes, if threatened, frogs scream and race towards their attacker, even if the attacker is many times bigger than themselves, like the size of a cat or even a person! It can be quite a surprise to be threatened by a frog puffed up and screeching!

MAKE A BOG

A bog is a great habitat for all kinds of wildlife. It is an area that many invertebrates go to drink and where birds will go to pick up a snack. A bog is ideally situated near a pond or a birdbath or the downpipe on a shed, anywhere that will top up the water level regularly and will mean that you don't need to add water specially to keep your bog wet.

Begin by digging out a shallow bowl in the soil about ten in (25 cm) deep in the middle and 2 ft (0.6 m) round. Pile the excavated soil onto a plastic sheet to make cleaning up easier. Smooth the bottom and sides of the hole and line it with plastic, then replace the soil that you dug out. The purpose isn't to make the hole water tight, just to slow the drainage to make a permanently damp area, not a sodden one. Gently soak the soil of your bog and keep watch. It won't be long before new life appears!

Pond dipping To go pond dipping you need to equip yourself with a very fine net, a shallow bowl or tray, a stickle jar, a magnifying glass and a good field guide. You need to use a very fine net because many of the creatures that live in your pond are far too small to be caught in an ordinary butterfly or rock pool net. Pond dipping nets can be found in shops that sell aquarium supplies or you can make your own by threading some old tights onto a wire hoop made from an old wire coat hanger. Push the ends into the hollow of a bamboo cane and bind it very tightly with string.

Fill your tray half full of pond water and place it next to you on a level surface. Now gently sweep your net through the water and lift it up. Carefully tip the contents of your net into the waiting tray and see what treasures you have found. You can transfer anything that needs closer examination into the stickle jar. Some of the really tiny

creatures can be placed in a drop of water onto a microscope slide and examined in detail, before you carefully place them back into the water. Some really exciting creatures can be kept for a day or two in a small fish tank inside, but remember your invertebrate pets need to eat and the pond water will get stale very quickly. Keep it fresh by removing half the water with a jug and tipping it back into the pond and topping it back up with fresh pond water. This needs to be done every day or your pond creatures will suffer, so it is usually better to make most of your investigations at the pond edge.

Any self-respecting witch in the olden days would have had to cultivate a good pond. Newts, like frogs and toads were an essential ingredient in many witches brews!

A Smooth newt may shed its skin as often as once a week.

NEWTS

Newts are charming amphibians that live part of their lives in the water and part out of the water. They are members of the salamander family and in some countries newts are called "salamanders" and salamanders are called "newts". If you find tadpoles in your pond, they may be newts, rather than frogs or toads. You can easily tell the difference; newts produce their front legs first and they grow large feathery gills that are very visible. Frogs and toads on the other hand develop their back legs first and they have no visible gills.

Many creatures feed on the tadpoles and young of newts, frogs and toads, including adult newts, frogs and toads!

The largest newt in Britain is the Great Crested Newt which is a registered endangered species. It grows to a rather modest 6 in (15 cm) long. His cousin, who lives on the island of Japan is rather larger. The Japanese giant salamander is a rather impressive 42 in (107 cm) long, that is over a yard (meter) in length, taller than most six year olds!

Smooth newt females lay their eggs on leaves in still water (rather than the running water of a stream or river). The mother newt lays her eggs and then carefully folds and glues the leaf edges together to protect it. If you inherit some pond plants from a friend or neighbour, you may well inherit a newt nursery as well.

Water spiders live their whole lives under water, although they still need to breathe air! These amazing arachnids spin a web under water, attached to stems of plants. They then swim to the water surface, trap a bubble of air and swim down to release it under the canopy of their web. They do this several times until they have a bubble large enough in which to live, to eat and to raise their babies.

There are also other spiders that spend their time on the water or hunting from leaves or the banks of the pond, but no others actually live in the water. Fishing spiders are found all over the world, and while some of them catch tiny fish, tadpoles and froglets, many others happily catch and eat the larva and adults of all the various types of invertebrates that can be found in your pond.

Some of the fishing spiders, like pond skater bugs, are able to skim over the 'skin' of the water, spreading their legs wide so as not to break the surface tension of the water.

Other pond creatures actually do the same thing, but upside-down, suspending themselves from the water surface as if they were hanging from a ceiling.

The larva of many invertebrates that inhabit your pond are equipped with gills that enable them to breathe beneath the surface. These gills disappear as the larva matures, so the adults have had to develop clever ways of breathing under water. The ferocious water scorpion has a long spine protruding from its rear that looks like a sharp sting; it is however a handy breathing tube that the bug pokes out into the air like a topsy-turvy snorkel. Some bugs trap tiny bubbles of air under their wing cases, while others collect bubbles on their body hair; sometimes so much air is collected that it is real struggle for the insect to descend beneath the surface as the trapped air acts like a float. When this happens the insect must struggle down with all its might, then cling to an underwater leaf or stalk to stop it from bobbing back up to the surface.

Caddis flies. There are many kinds of caddis flies, and some of them are particularly fun to observe because of the way they dress! The larval stages camouflage themselves by spinning a coat made of spit and whatever they fancy! They use an ingenious underwater glue to stick grains of sand, tiny stones and bits of plants to their silk coat to camouflage themselves in the water. The glue they use is so amazing that scientists are studying it to find out if they can use it to help doctors stick peoples' insides together during surgery!

Little Miss Muffet who sat on her tuffet is thought to be a reference to the stepdaughter of Dr Thomas Muffet who was an entomologist 400 years ago. He is said to have dosed his poor Mary with ground up spiders when she was ill. Not surprisingly she developed a dreadful fear of spiders. The practice of using spiders as medicine isn't as unusual as it sounds. Spiders, fresh or dried have been used in Europe and the Americas to cure malaria, toothache and many other illnesses. Poor spiders!

Dragonflies and Damselflies
belong to the insect group called "*Odonata*". This is a clue to how they eat, as *Odonata* means "toothed jaws". Dragonflies are super fliers, and can fly at 38 kmph (24 mph). They can manoeuvre and steer so well because each set of wings moves independently in a figure of eight. This lets them turn, start and stop with precision. Their eyes take up almost all of their heads, and each one has as many as 30,000 separate lenses; no wonder they are so hard to sneak up on! Dragonflies and damselflies live their adult live in the air and this stage only lasts from between two to six weeks, but they spend their young lives under water which can last as long as five years!

Scientists have found fossils which show that giant dragonflies with wings 2 ft (60 cm) across inhabited the earth 300 million years ago, that is even before the dinosaurs!

That's my great-grand-daddy

UNDERGROWTH AND OLD WOOD

A DEAD LOG FOR CREEPY CRAWLIES

Dead wood is everywhere. If you know of an old log that is lying somewhere in the sun, ask permission to move it; the log would likely be put to greater good if it was carefully sited in a semi-shady spot and given your special attention. Dig a hole deep enough to anchor your log upright in the soil. Firm the soil around the base of the log and get drilling. Use a hand drill to excavate large and small holes in the top and sides of the log. Leave some of these holes empty, ready to accommodate visitors, but in others add some straw containing old chicken manure or a handful of rotted compost. This will begin the process

of decay and adds lovely nutrients at the same time, mimicking the conditions in a woodland where bird droppings and old leaves would litter the logs as they fall.

You can make your log or your logpile as fancy or as simple as you want. You will be creating a home for all sorts of creatures that love the dark and the damp and the safety of a woody pile. If you are lucky you could find mice and shrews, toads and frogs, snakes and slow worms alongside all the busy beetles, slugs and woodlice, millipedes and centipedes who will move in.

Most snails, like worms, are hermaphrodites, which means they have both male and female reproductive organs. To mate and lay eggs two snails sidle up alongside each other and when they are close they each shoot a dart into the other snails' side. This dart contains the sperm which fertilizes the eggs contained within the snails. Because they are snails the whole thing is done in slow motion and is really easy to watch. When they have finished, each snail is able to go off and lay a clutch of eggs in the soil or under a damp log.

Fungi are everywhere and they come in as many shapes, sizes and colors as the flowers in your garden. Fungi are also essential for the health of your garden. Without them working away at breaking down the plant material and turning it into new soil, we would be buried under the remains of fallen trees and old plants. Scientists are now finding out that the *mycelium*—fungal threads—that run through the soil, are so important that if they are destroyed by too much digging, the soil will die and won't be able to support the growth of food or flowers.

Purseweb spiders are truly scary hunters, if you are the size of a beetle, that is! Purseweb spiders line a hole in the ground with a silken tube that juts out at the top. When a prey insect wanders across the web the spider pounces, piercing the insect through the silk and dragging it down to its lair. Finding a purseweb spider in your woody corner is a great privilege and a treat to be able to examine its intricate architecture!

What do you call a very old ant? An antique!

DUST/ANT BATH

A patch of dry earth, especially if there is an ant's nest near-by, is a great attraction to birds who will visit it to have a good clean-up. Birds will roll and flap in the dirt, flicking the dust and any stray ants over their feathers. The furious ants will squirt formic acid over the bird as a defence. This is just what the bird wants, as the stinging spray will drive away any irritating pests like lice or fleas.

Ants all belong to a group of invertebrate called "social insects" which means they live together in colonies, rather than as individuals. These colonies can be set up in many parts of your garden, but they are perhaps most noticeable when, on one hot sunny day in summer, all the ants in the neighbourhood take to the air in a mating flight. In early afternoon, the time and the weather will trigger both the large female and the smaller males to fly up, where they will mate on the wing and then return to ground. The females will now go off to start a new colony as queens and the males will return to their old nests to carry on as before.

Some ants, like the fierce and feisty three-waisted red ants, rely on their stings for defence, while others like black ants and the two-waisted reds use their sharp jaws and acidic spray to defend their territories. If you should accidently disturb a colony of ants watch for a moment the frantic activity as everyone is deployed to protect the larvae, pupae and eggs, snatching them up in their jaws and carrying them off to safety. It takes only minutes for the entire population to decamp to a new nest. What co-operation!

Chuggypigs, sowbugs, cheesy bugs, doodlebugs as well as the little pillbugs who rejoice in the scientific name of **Armadillidium** ("ar-ma-dill-id-ee-um") are all woodlice. There are many different kinds of woodlice, as well as a type of pill millipede that looks just like a pill bug, but is no relation. Make a collection and see how many different types you can find.

TO MAKE A CHUGGY PIG-STY

You will need:

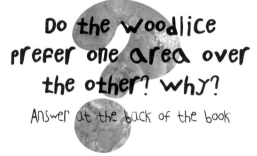

Do the woodlice prefer one area over the other? why?

Answer at the back of the book

- A shoe box or plant tray

- Some newspaper or kitchen roll

- Some water and some chuggypigs.

1. For an experiment line the bottom of a shoe box or plant tray with newspaper and carefully pour a small amount of water on to it, so that half of the paper is damp and half is dry.

2. Now catch a dozen woodlice and place them in the box. To make it a fair test, make sure that the bottom of the box is evenly lit, with no dark corners.

woodlice are more closely related to shrimps than to the worms and beetles with whom they share their home.

SNAKES

You would be very lucky to find any type of snake in your garden unless you live in the countryside. If they do venture into your garden they may search out the safety of a woodpile and they also like the winter warmth of a compost heap, and may choose to lay their eggs there, in the snug darkness in spring. The longest wild snake in Britain is the grass snake; one measured up at a whopping 6 foot (nearly 2 m) long while in North America the Eastern Indigo has been found at an impressive 9 foot (nearly 3 m) long.

One naturalist is well known for his method of monitoring the snakes on his patch; he lays down squares of corrugated metal, painted black. Snakes frequently rest up under these squares because they are sheltered and warm. The dark metal absorbs the heat of the sun and transfers it to the snake underneath.

Daddy, are we poisonous?

Of course we are son, why do you ask?

Cause I've just bitten my tongue!

Snakes were once said to make you invisible; on a certain night of the year when all the planets were aligned above the earth you were advised to catch, kill, skin and dry a snake. crushed to a powder and held in your hand, it was believed that you would turn invisible.

WALLS AND FENCES

Keep your eyes peeled for signs of the life that exists at the base of a wall or under a roof. There is a whole world waiting to be discovered in the cracks and crevices of walls and fences and under the eaves of sheds and houses. Creatures that would once have lived and hunted in the natural habitats of rocky cliffs, stony banks and on standing dead wood now spend their lives on the man-made vertical surfaces of our homes and gardens. You can make a crumbling wall or a fence post even more welcoming by adding nest boxes and feeding posts.

Make a bee post. An offcut of wood with shallow holes drilled into it makes an excellent place for solitary bees, like mason bees, to lay their eggs. Make sure the holes are between 0.1 and 0.5 in (0.2 and 1.2 cm) in diameter. Hang it on a fence or on a wall of your home.

Make a bee lodge by drilling deep holes lengthwise into a variety of logs, but make sure the entrance holes are smooth and free of sawdust as the bees that choose this type of lodging are fussy about their front doors.

Walls are a great place to hang your nest boxes, and birds aren't the only ones to appreciate a cosy place to raise their families. **Bats** also need a warm, safe roost and as they hibernate as well, a bat box placed high on a house wall would serve two purposes at once. See page 83 on instructions about how to make a bat box.

If you are ever lost in the woods you will always know which way is north if you look out for lichen (pronounced "like-in") and moss growing on tree trunks; it tends to grow more thickly on the north side. Lichens are an ingenious combination of two different organisms, fungi and algae, that work together to do different jobs.

LICHENS AND MOSSES

When you come across some **moss or lichen** growing on walls, trees or fences, get out your magnifying glass because they are worth a closer look. There are thousands of different types of mosses, some weird and wonderful, some beautiful. Moss don't have real roots and they don't flower, but they do produce spores (like seeds) from delicate little lanterns called **sporangia** ("spore-ang-jee-a").

Lichens grow incredibly slowly and are used to find out how long some structures have been standing, so if a stone has a 1.25 in (3 cm) patch of lichen that only grows 0.4 in (1 cm) every 50 years, scientists will know that the structure has been standing there for at least 150 years!

How clean is it in your neighbourhood? Lichens are also a good measure of air pollution, most lichens only grow where the air is clear and pure.

They are also incredibly tough. In 2002 scientists sent a sample of lichen up into space and left it unprotected and exposed to the huge fluctuations of heat and cold and to the cosmic space rays and then they brought it back to earth, where it lived!

what do you call a really big swallow?

A gulp.

It was once thought that swallows flew all the way up to the moon in the winter months to bide their time until the return of summer. Even more bizarre, some of the cleverest men of the time believed that swallows hibernated beneath the waves in lakes.

SWIFTS, HOUSE MARTINS AND SWALLOWS

All of these birds feed on insects on the wing so you won't see them at your bird table, but if you are lucky enough to have a large pond which is lively with flying insects, you may get evening visits from hungry swallows or be entertained by the overhead acrobatics of these super swoopers.

If you live in a town or a rural area you could encourage these special visitors to breed on your patch. While you would be very lucky to entice a swift to nest under the eaves of your house or in the rafters of an old shed, you may well be able to play host to the occasional House Martin family. If you put up an artificial nest this may encourage a pair to choose your eaves as a suitable nesting site, they may not actually choose your nest, but it could give them the idea that it is a desirable neighbourhood, worth moving into. Other things you can do is to have a ready supply of mud for their house building; your boggy patch would do the job nicely. And if you have a large pond, the flying insects would go some way to helping the house martins to feed their young.

Swallows rarely land unless they are nesting. They eat, mate and even sleep while they are flying! Amazingly they manage to rest by sleeping on one side of their brain at a time, and then switching over to rest the other side. They routinely stay in the air for more than three years without touching the ground even once!

MAKE A HOUSE MARTIN'S NEST

You will need:

- **A ball about 7 in (18 cm) in diameter**

- **Large scissors**

- **Dried mud or plaster of Paris**

- **Chopped up straw**

- **Two L-shaped brackets**

- **Piece of wood 0.5 in (1.5 cm) thick and about 9 in (23 cm) square.**

Cut the ball into quarters; this will give you four nests. In one of the quarters, cut an entrance hole on the top edge which measures 1 in (2.5 cm) deep by 2.5 in (6 cm) wide. Now cover the outside of the ball with an 0.3 in (0.8 cm) layer of dried mud or plaster of Paris mixed with straw. Fix the ball to a piece of wood with an L-shaped bracket and ask an adult to attach it under the eaves of the house.

Swallows may nest near you if you have an open porch or a garage with a permanently open window. Swallows like to build their mud and straw nests on the ledges high inside quiet buildings. A swallows nest is constructed much the same as a house martins nest, but without the entrance hole, swallows like to use their nests like a cup.

what British mammal used to be called a flitter mouse?

Answer at the back of the book.

The tiny hearts of pygmy shrews can beat at 1,200 beats per minute (yours only beats at about 90 beats per minute) and they have been known to die of fright! They don't like loud noises so move slowly and carefully if you see a shrew and keep very quiet!

MOUSE, VOLE OR SHREW?

You can tell the difference between mice voles and shrews by the shapes of their noses. The long wiffly noses of shrews point to them needing to search out scurrying and wriggling insects. Mice are omnivorous and will eat seeds, insects, worms and even carrion. Voles have blunt noses and they eat berries, leaves, seeds and some insects, they need more water than mice so they aren't quite so fond of seeds as their neighbours.

Shrews commonly nest in the cracks and crevices at the base of walls and under sheds. These tiny animals are mainly insectivorous and are a great help to the wildlife gardener as they are rather fond of slugs, beetle larvae and other ground dwelling beasties, however they are ferocious hunters and they have also been known to catch and eat mice!

Pigmy shrews are the smallest mammals in the world and they can weigh as little as a penny coin. Amazingly they have a poisonous bite which they use to subdue their prey when hunting.

Shrews aren't all fierce and feisty; they also have the charming habit of caravanning, when a mother shrew wants to move her babies they all travel in a line, each grasping the base of the tail of the one in front. That way they don't get lost in the undergrowth.

Mice and voles generally live for no longer than two years, which seems like a very short little life. However if you think that these delightful rodents grow from tiny naked babies to fully-grown adults, able to breed and raise their own families in just six weeks then it doesn't seem quite so short!

Mice tend to move around their territory in leaps and bounds while voles aren't quite so acrobatic, and are more likely to scurry and run; keep this in mind when you are trying to figure out who's who in the undergrowth. Some mice, like wood mice and the larger yellow-necked mice, are as much at home on the branches of trees as they are in a corner of your garden shed or in a burrow underground, and they will happily hide their store of nuts and berries in an empty birds' nest 30 ft (10 m) above the ground.

How many voles do you think there are there in Britain?

Answer at the back of the book

What did the mummy mouse say to the baby mouse?

Squeak when you're spoken too.

Mice, shrews and voles are very active and often use the same pathways to negotiate their way around their territory, and it isn't unusual for them to wear away a miniature highway beneath the grasses. You may be able to spot the tiny path but you would have to know your garden very well! However there may be another way. Many small rodents have ultraviolet pee! Unfortunately we humans can't see ultraviolet, but with careful observations and the help of a special black light torch you may just be able to make out the trails and scent marks of your tiny neighbours. Some of the predators that hunt these tiny rodents, like kestrels and buzzards, do have the ability to see ultraviolet and can detect, from very high up, the trails left by their dinner, just as if they were sign posts saying "come and get me!" Unfortunately cats can also see ultraviolet.

LIZARDS

Lizards will make use of many areas of your garden, but they are, perhaps, most often spotted disappearing between the stones or bricks of old walls. And while they like the safety of walls, they also love to sunbathe. Because they are cold-blooded they need the warmth of the sun to give them energy in-between feasting. Choose a dark coloured rock (the darker the better, in order to absorb the heat from the sun) and prop it up in the sun but close to the safety of your wall.

IN THE NIGHT GARDEN

Some animals always visit when you aren't around, but it can be exciting to know they are there, nonetheless. A great way to check out visitors is by laying a footprint trap. It takes patience, but if you are able to clear a space near a wall, a bird feeder, a compost heap or a log pile, you are very likely to spot the evidence of the nocturnal life in your garden.

You can make night-time observations by inserting a small solar-powered lamp into the ground near your feeding station. These inexpensive lamps cast just enough light to let you identify your visitors, and to enjoy their antics.

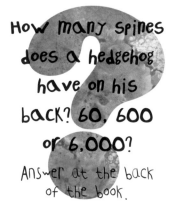

How many spines does a hedgehog have on his back? 60, 600 or 6,000? Answer at the back of the book.

Begin by clearing a space about 18 in (46 cm) square and levelling it. On top of this spread a smooth layer of sand or sieved earth. The reason you need to sieve the earth is because the footprints of the animals you are likely to attract will be very small. If the earth is lumpy or hard you won't be able to see any tracks and your trap won't work. Begin by placing a small amount of tempting food in the center of the clearing, seeds are always a treat for small mammals such as wood mice, and small worms and slugs are always on the menu for shrews with their lovely wiffly

noses. To restrict the menu to very small creatures you can make a tiny table out of four small stones with a large flat stone or a square of wood balanced on the top. This will enable the little guys to get to the food and provide protection from marauding cats. Make sure you make the 'table' very stable so it doesn't end in tragedy if the top becomes dislodged and falls on the diners! It may take some time to attract visitors to your feeding station, but one morning when you go to check your trap, you will notice footprints in the earth, a good guide will help you identify the various prints.

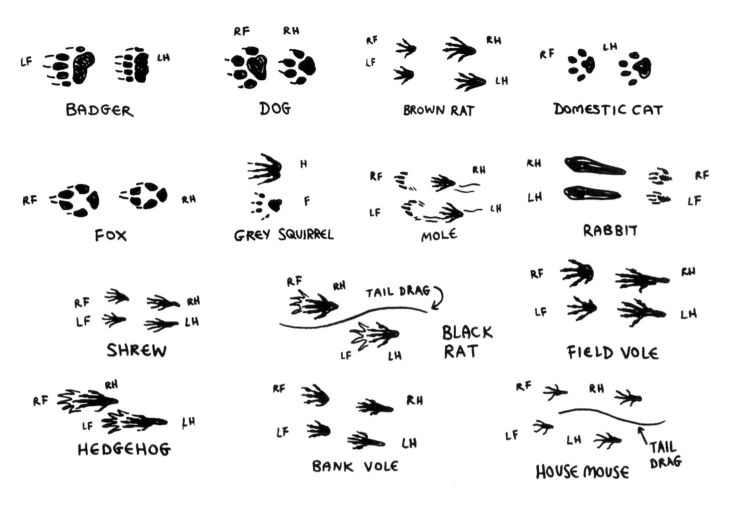

GO HUNTING BY TORCHLIGHT.

Equip yourself with a flashlight (torch), soft-soled shoes, quiet clothes and a couple of collecting pots and go out hunting in the dark. Late in the evening on a hot summers' day is the best time for night hunting. Creeping around your garden with a torch will reveal, not only who is out and about in the darkness, but how the day-time creatures behave at night. What do they do, where do they go? For an active hunt begin by peering at the undersides of leaves and into bushes. Tread slowly and carefully. Can you find bees and wasps sleeping in the cool of the night? Some bees spend the dark hours suspended from leaf or flower stalks, and so wrapped up in the world of sleep that they will not stir even if you disturb their perch. Head for the flower border and investigate who you can spot sipping at the nectar bar. The grass will still be busy with daddy longlegs, spiders and the various moisture loving animals like slugs and snails who use the night to travel around the garden without fear of bird

attack or heat of the sun. Point your torch skywards; can you spot the flit of a bat, the flutter of a passing moth, or even the shadow of an owls.

There are all sorts of sounds that can be investigated with a little patience, from the night song of crickets and cicadas to the croaking of frogs looking for mates. Some birds sing at night and if you are still and quiet you may be able to spot one trilling in the branches of a tree. In city gardens birds tend to sing into the night to avoid having to compete with the cacophony of sounds from industry and traffic. Train your ears to locate the sounds around you and when there is something close by, switch on the torch and track down the source.

Moths are the typical night-visitor to gardens and what's more, they are easily enticed up close by the simple use of light. It's a bit odd that night fliers such as moths are attracted to light. If light is all that great to a moth why don't we see them around during the day and find them sleeping at night? Some entomologists think that because moths navigate by the moon, they become confused when there is another bright light shining in the darkness. Other entomologists think that moths mistake lights for the ultraviolet reflection of the moon's glow on flower petals so they approach the light believing they are going to settle down to a lovely drink of nectar!

Remember to free your moths in the same place that you caught them.

TO MAKE A MOTH TRAP

You will need:

- **A large white sheet**

- **Strings and clothes pegs**

- **A powerful flashlight (torch)**

- **A field guide which includes moths, a butterfly net**

- **A selection of collecting jars**

- **A camera with a flash.**

1. To make your trap simply rig up a white sheet by tying it between the branches of a tree or pegging it on a washing line. Place your flashlight (torch) behind the sheet so the light shines through it and wait for the moths to appear.

2. Time how long it takes until the first one arrives. If you like the idea of studying moths but aren't keen on the fluttering, simply put on a broad-brimmed hat and a long sleeved shirt, but if you like to get up really close make sure you are wearing the whitest shirt you own and stand right next to the glowing sheet when the action really starts, you can be your own moth magnet! Make sure someone is standing by with a camera to capture the fun.

3. Carefully trap some of the most common or the most interesting moths in your jars to make identification easier. Once you have collected all you need, take the jars inside so that you can see the details of your specimens properly. When you identify them, try asking yourself why you were able to trap this particular moth in your garden: are you growing one of its foods, or perhaps the food its larva feed on. Does your garden play some essential part in the lifecycle of this moth? Try setting your trap on several evenings and record your results, then try leaving it for several weeks and trying again. Will you catch the same species? Why?

where you live will determine who visits your garden after dark; different ecosystems support different creatures.

In North America racoons and skunks are not uncommon visitors to gardens and, while adults dislike the mess raccoons make when they root around in their garbage bins and run rampant through their fruit bushes, kids rather enjoy the noisy, comical antics of a troop of mischievous raccoons. Skunks are very beneficial visitors to large gardens, where they eat grubs and slugs with noisy relish, provided you keep any pets indoors and are able to view them from behind the safety of a window! If you live in the country or on the edge of a large town you may even be lucky enough to have an occasional visit from a slow and steady porcupine; because they are so slow and lumbering, porcupines pose no threat to people, however over-curious pets need to be kept away from their wickedly sharp spines!

Do hedgehogs live wild in North America?

Answer at the back of the book!

Just like little humans, little hedgehogs have baby teeth which fall out to be replaced by adult teeth.

Are hedgehogs and porcupines related?

Answer at the back of the book.

Can a porcupine or a hedgehog shoot their quills?

Neither; porcupines are easily able to drop their quills but they don't have the ability to shoot them out. Hedgehogs on the other hand are very attached to their spines and they are not easily removed.

In Britain hedgehogs are frequent night time visitors. Often they have a route that takes them through several gardens, and if yours is one of them you may well hear them snuffling and scuffling in the undergrowth. Hedgehogs are a gardener's friend as they are voracious slug hunters, and you can encourage them to keep coming back by giving them a snack of cat or dog food in a shallow saucer each night. Some people give them bread and milk but sadly this will give them tummy ache, so if you are going to feed them, stick to good quality pet food instead. Remember if you see a nocturnal animal out during the day it is most likely not well. Keep your eye on it for a little while and if it doesn't seek out a dark corner in which to shelter, it would be a good idea to take it along to a wildlife rescue center for some attention.

If you are lucky enough to hear a hedgehog snuffling around in the undergrowth of your garden during the warmer months, it would be a great help to make a shelter for it to hibernate in over the winter. Make sure you build it in good time so your visitor knows it is there, ready for when it is needed. (see page 84)

FOXES

Foxes are the most widespread wild land mammal on earth. Like us, they are omnivorous, which means that they eat just about anything. Foxes used only to be seen in the countryside but they have learnt that there is a good living to be had in towns and cities where they will scavenge for left-overs as well as enjoy meals put out for them by kindly people. It isn't unusual to see a fox family emerging from under an old shed in the spring. Foxes only use their 'earths' until late spring or early summer, after which they sleep above ground in thickets or dense vegetation. In very early spring female foxes, called vixens, can be heard screeching a mating call—a sound that can be quite terrifying the first time you hear it—and being answered by the bark of the dog fox. Cat or dog food will attract hedgehogs and foxes, especially if it is left out every night. In North America, skunks and racoons will take the place of hedgehogs, so beware!

Feeding foxes, like feeding any wild animal, needs to be done with care. Don't try to feed huge amounts to your fox every night, as foxes are territorial and if they do most of their eating in your garden they won't try to defend a larger area. This could mean that if you stop feeding for any reason, your fox will have a very small area in which to look for food. Try not to encourage your fox to lose its fear of humans, not everyone would be pleased to be approached by a fox, and he might come to some harm.

Foxes have been known to gently select the ripest and tastiest berries from a blackberry bush, with their lips!

OWLS

A hoot or a screech is probably the only indication you will get that an owl is in your neighbourhood. The trick is knowing which kind of owl has come visiting. Different owls have different calls, and different habits, some being nocturnal, some diurnal and some crepuscular.

The tawny owl is the most likely visitor to gardens as they have adapted to live anywhere where there are trees—parks, gardens and woodlands will suit them equally well. It is the tawny owl who calls "twit-twoo". A female calls "too-whit" and the male answers "too-wooo". Their calls can be both a comfort and a thrill if you hear them when you are tucked up in bed and they are busy patrolling the countryside.

The familiar soft "hoo-hoo" call is the sound of a male long-eared owl who hunts only at night and is rarely seen, while the harsh scary "screech" that can make you jump is the haunting cry of the barn owl.

They are mad, alright.

The poor old owl was once used, suitably prepared, as a cure for madness, epilepsy and to improve poor eyesight!

"what do you call an owl with a low voice?"" A growl!"

WHAT DOES A MOTHER BAT FEED HER NEW BORN BABY?

Answer at the back of the book

Bats hibernate in groups called colonies. They are able to hang upside down for long periods because unlike ourselves, a bat's feet are clenched when they are relaxed.

What's the best way to hold a bat?

By the handle!

worldwide, almost 1/4 of all mammals are bats!

BATS

Bats are a wonderful measure of a healthy garden. If you regularly see Bats flying about at dusk you can be sure that your garden supports a healthy insect population so give yourself a pat on the back, you have made a terrific wildlife haven.

Most bats around the world find their food by echolocation; by letting out a high pitched shout, they use their large ears to read the sound waves as they are bounced back off the insects flying in front of them. They can even read how big the insect is and in which direction it is flying, and they can do all that so quickly that they still have time to catch it before it flies away!

Size for size, bats produce the largest babies of all mammals. A pipistrelle can give birth to a baby that is already a quarter of her size, that is the same as a human mother giving birth to a baby that is the size of the average four year old!

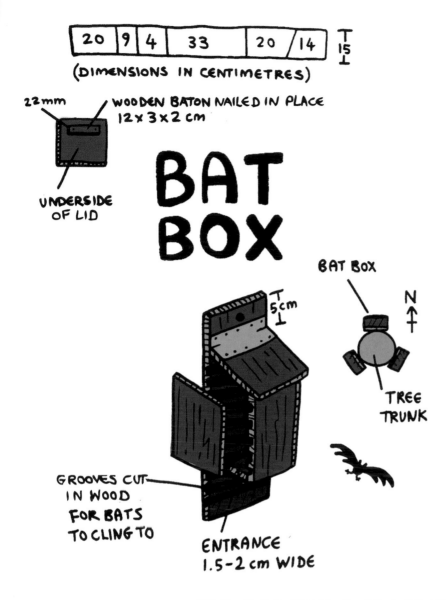

| 20 | 9 | 4 | 33 | 20 | 14 | T 15 |

(DIMENSIONS IN CENTIMETRES)

22mm

WOODEN BATON NAILED IN PLACE
12 x 3 x 2 cm

UNDERSIDE
OF LID

BAT BOX

BAT BOX

T 5cm

N ↑

TREE TRUNK

GROOVES CUT
IN WOOD
FOR BATS
TO CLING TO

ENTRANCE
1.5-2 cm WIDE

THE 1-2-3 OF BEAUTIFUL BATS

Make a variety of habitats such as a wet area, a shrubby area, and a mini-meadow. Remember, none of these need to be vast, even a small pond or a single small tree will support an enormous variety of insects and other creatures. Don't use chemicals in your garden.

Put up a night light, preferably solar powered, somewhere up high such as in a tree or on a post in the garden to encourage night-flying insects which will attract bats.

Plant night-scented flowers along with your other plants; group them in a clump rather than dotted around the beds and borders so that moths and other nocturnal insects can find them easily. See page 90 for a list of night-scented flowers.

Place a comfy seat in a spot where you can see the comings and goings of your night garden.

One tiny pipistrelle bat, weighing no more than four grams can eat over 3000 (yes, three thousand!) insects in one night.

TO MAKE A BAT BOX

You will need:

- A plank of pine or larch or other untreated scrap wood measuring 43 in (110 cm) long , 6 in (15 cm) wide and 1 in (2 cm) thick

- A scrap of leather or vinyl measuring 2 by 6 in (5 by 15 cm)

- A ruler or tape measure, a drill, a saw and 30 pin nails.

Bats don't have tape measures, so you can use any untreated wood of similar dimensions, as long as it is thick enough to insulate your bats against the heat and the cold.

1. Cut the plank into the lengths as illustrated on the diagram.

2. Cut grooves into the backboard to act as a gripper board for the bats to cling to.

3. Assemble the box by nailing the pieces together. Make the top joint waterproof by nailing the strip of vinyl over the join.

4. Drill a hole at the top of the box to allow you to attach your bat box to a tree or wall.

5. Choose your bat site carefully, hanging the box between 3 and 5 yards (3 and 5 m) above ground, out of the wind and direct sun. If you can, build several boxes and place them facing different directions so that your bats can have roosts for different seasons.

WINTER GARDENS

Many mammals hibernate in the cold months of winter when food is scarce. During hibernation animals drop their body temperature and slow their heart rate so that their bodies don't require so much nourishment. To survive through the cold without food they need somewhere warm and safe and dry. You can help by supplying some animals—from bees to bats—with cosy winter homes.

You will need:

- A sturdy wooden or heavy duty cardboard box at least 18 in (45cm) square

- A square of heavy duty plastic large enough to cover the top and sides of the box

- A supply of dry leaves, straw and thin twigs

- Leafy branches— the prunings from evergreen hedges are ideal.

MAKE A HIBERNATION HUT

1. Begin by cutting a 6 in (15 cm) doorway in one side of the box. Drill a few small air holes around the sides for ventilation.

2. Place your hut in an out-of-the-way corner of the garden where it will be sheltered from cold winter winds. Cover the hut with the plastic and surround it with twigs and leafy branches. Make sure the plastic is held firmly in place and cannot blow around and startle your guests. Now push a couple of handfuls of dry leaves inside to begin the makings of the bed and leave the rest outside so your guest can finish the job himself.

3. Animals often move house if they wake up during warm spells during hibernation, so if you have the space and you really want to encourage winter visitors, try making a village of two or three huts, spaced around the garden.

what did the hedgehog say when he put his coat on inside out?

OUCH!

If you are lucky you may see some evidence of someone taking up residence; keep a look out, but resist the temptation to keep checking close-up because they may just decide to go elsewhere if it is too busy. Your guests will begin to emerge from their winter hideaways when their food becomes available again and the temperatures are on the rise.

In North America chipmunks and other small mammals often build their homes beneath the safety and shelter of a pile of brushwood. You can make a perfect winter shelter for them with nothing but scraps from your garden. Begin by saving any twiggy branches from pruned shrubs and trees. Lay these on the ground in a sheltered corner of your garden and continue adding to your brushwood pile in a criss-cross fashion; this will make the pile good and strong. As winter approaches, gather the falling leaves and spread them over your pile in thick layers and finish off by arranging some heavier branches and logs on the top to prevent any larger mammals from trying to dig out your winter lodgers. Keep an ear tuned for the sounds of animals busily preparing for winter.

Don't be too quick to clean up the hollow stems and old seed heads of summer plants are perfect hibernaculums for mini-beasts and a good winter food source for birds.

Bumblebees are active very late in the autumn and very early in the spring; you may even see them bumbling about on Christmas Day if the weather is warm. Make sure you provide a little bit of food for a mid-winter snack by planting flowers that produce nectar at this time of year. *Viburnum tinus* and *Viburnum bodnantense*, winter heathers, primroses and winter aconites may be a life saver at this time of year. See the planting lists at the back of the book for more ideas.

Only the queen bumblebee lives through the winter and so only she hibernates. She will search out a spot under some dry moss, in a grassy thicket or under a pile of leaves. If you uncover a sleepy bee nestled in the undergrowth in winter, tuck her back up and leave her to continue her sleep until the spring.

Watch out for butterflies hibernating in the corners of sheds, garages or even inside the house in winter. Some butterflies and moths pass the winter as pupae, their cocoons buried safely in the garden soil but several butterflies 'over-winter' as adults. You may discover a motionless butterfly in a corner. Check on it from time to time and when the weather warms up watch as it appears to come to life again. Only let it outside if spring has really arrived otherwise it will perish if the weather turns cold again.

If you find an active butterfly in the house in winter, capture it gently and place it in a shoe box in a cool room out of direct sunlight until it is safe to release it outside.

Some butterflies and other mini-beasts contain a chemical called glycol that stops their blood freezing in the bitterly cold weather of winter, the same stuff that stops the water in our cars freezing solid!

Ladybirds and lacewings are the gardeners' friend; they eat the aphids, greenfly and blackfly that suck the life out of our plants and spread plant diseases. You can welcome adult ladybirds and lacewings into your garden and keep them there by providing them with a warm, dry place to spend the winter.

TO MAKE A LADYBIRD AND LACEWING LODGE

You will need:

- A large tin with one end neatly cut away

- Several pieces of bamboo cane

- A selection of thin, hollow twigs.

1. Fill the tin with lengths of bamboo; they don't all need to be the same size but they shouldn't stick out much beyond the rim of the tin.

2. Push the twigs into the hollows between the bamboo canes. Let some of them stick out a bit so that the ladybirds and lacewings have somewhere to land.

3. Push the lodge securely, with the opening pointing slightly downwards, into an evergreen hedge or a dense shrub and leave it undisturbed.

Birds need to be fed in the winter and a large variety of seeds, berries and fats are the best things to offer them at this time of year. Suet balls are terrific for providing energy and protein but grated mild cheese, peanut butter, cake crumbs, pieces of fresh or dried fruit, cooked potatoes and rice are all great additions to the bird table, and the bonus is that many of these are things that wouldn't be put in the compost heap, so you are doing even more recycling while you are feeding your birds.

You can get very creative by making and baking bird cakes as a winter treat for your birds.

You will need:

- **Suet**

- **Bird seed**

- **A saucepan**

- **Wooden spoon**

- **Disposable plastic cup (or other shaped moulds)**

- **Some thick string.**

TO MAKE WARMING WINTER TREATS FOR YOUR BIRDS

1. Gently melt a cup of suet over a low heat.

2. When the suet has liquefied, add a cup of mixed bird seed and stir it well until combined. Allow it to cool in the saucepan for at least 15 minutes.

3. Tie a thick, bulky knot in one end of the string and rest the knot in the bottom of the plastic cup. Slowly spoon or pour the seed/suet mix into the cup and leave it until it hardens.

4. Once it is cold and solid, remove the bird cake from the cup by squeezing gently. Take your bird treat out and hang it up within sight of a window, then sit back and watch the fun!

Don't be disappointed if you don't immediately get a huge number of birds visiting your table, you need to give it time for word to get around. A few live mealworms from the live-food section of a pet shop will often kick start the process, especially on a sunny day when the wriggling of the worms will catch the eye of passing birds.

Try making a winter bird list, unless you know what to look out and listen for, you may miss some of the shyer visitors to your garden. Pay a visit to nearby wildlife sanctuaries or get in touch with local natural history groups for information about customary winter bird populations in your area. In Kansas the **Cedar Waxwing** is the typical winter bird while in New York the bright red **Cardinal** is the bird everyone associates with winter.

Robins are the gardeners' companion and in Britain they are especially noticeable in winter. They soon recognize the signs of digging in the garden, when they will perch nearby, often very close indeed, ready to feast on uncovered grubs or worms. Male robins are fiercely territorial, fighting any rival males who enter their patch, and even displaying and attacking their own reflection in a mirror or a scrap of red fabric! North American and European robins are not related. The larger American robin is a member of the thrush family and the European robin is believed to be related to fly-catchers.

what kind of bird should you never take to the bank?

▲ robin!

TEN OF THE BEST PLANT LISTS FOR EVERY PURPOSE

Ten really quick-growing trees and large shrubs:

sycamore, hazel, ash, buddleia, birch, willow, elder, crab apple, larch, leylandii.

Ten plants for winter berries:

holly, mahonia, pyracantha, cotoneaster, viburnum tinus, dog rose, hawthorn, mountain ash, ivy, berberis.

Ten plants for seeds:

teasel, dandelion, thistle, sunflower, goldenrod, evening primrose, ornamental grasses, clematis, Michaelmas daisy, rosa rugosa.

Ten plants for nectar:

honeysuckle, bistort (*Polygonum superbum*), verbena bonariensis, buddleia, sedum, marigold, geranium, yarrow, fennel, calendula (pot marigold).

Ten all-purpose plants that do lots of different jobs:

buddleia, elder, crabapple, ivy, rosa rugosa, lavender, marjoram, sunflower, plum tree, honeysuckle.

Ten yummy, scrummy herbs to attract bees, butterflies, hoverflies and lacewings:

lavender, parsley, marjoram, rosemary, chive, pot marigold, fennel, dill, borage, sage.

Ten night-scented plants to encourage moths and bats:

evening primrose, flowering tobacco (*Nicotiana alata* or *affinis*), night scented stock, honeysuckle, white jasmine, red valerian, single pink, soapwort, campions, hemp agrimony.

Ten of the best meadow flowers:

annual cornflower, oxeye daisy, cowslips, ragged robin, red campion, harebell, wild marjoram, chicory, viper's bugloss, clover.

Some of the best bee plants:

try to plant a selection that will provide a meal all the year round. SPRING—fruit tree blossoms, lungwort (pulmonaria), primroses, cranesbills (geraniums). SUMMER—vipers bugloss, white and red clover, honeysuckle. AUTUMN—asters and Michaelmas daisy, sedum autumn joy, blue flowered sages and salvias. WINTER—mahonia, aconite, heathers and ling, hellebores, winter flowering honeysuckle (*lonicera fragrantissima*).

QUIZ ANSWERS

Do the woodlice prefer one area over the other?

Woodlice don't just like damp corners, they need them! Woodlice breathe through gills, like fish, not lungs, like we do, so they need water in tiny quantities in order to breathe.

How many voles are there in Britain?

100 million!

How many eyes does a fly have?

Flies only have two eyes, but each one has around 4,000 lenses, as opposed to our eyes which have only one each!

How long is the longest earth worm in the world?

Some earthworms can reach lengths of 22 ft (7m); that is as long as a stretch limousine.

What makes it so difficult for a robin to pull a slippery earthworm out of the soil?

Worms are equipped with tiny hairs which can grip the soil and with exceptional strength—they are about 1,000 times stronger than humans, size for size, that is!

How many legs does a centipede really have?

A centipede may have 100 feet, or as few as 30! How about a millipede? Between 36 and 200, not 1,000 as their name says!

How many spines does a hedgehog have on his back?

6,000!

What does a mother bat feed her new born baby?

Bats are mammals, and like all mammals, they feed their babies on milk until they are old enough to make the trip out of their roost.

What British mammal used to be called a flitter mouse?

Bats, because they look a little like mice and can flitter and flutter like birds.

Do hedgehogs live wild in North America?

No, there are no native hedgehogs in North America, but there is a trend towards keeping hedgehogs as pets, just like rabbits or guinea pigs!

Are hedgehogs and porcupines related?

No, despite looking similar, porcupines are rodents, like rats, while hedgehogs are not. Porcupines are vegetarian and hedgehogs are omnivores.

What job did pigeons have during the Second World War?

Pigeons were used in the Second World War to carry secret messages; but hawks were also used by the other side to catch and kill these secret agents before they could deliver the message. This wasn't a new practice, the Sultan of Bagdad used messenger pigeons 1,000 years ago!

Why garden without peat?

Centuries ago plants died and fell into soggy swamps, where they decayed and changed into a substance that resembles soil. The trouble is that peat bogs are very sensitive places and, if they are dug up they can't re-grow. There are loads of fascinating things that are unique to peat bogs. In fact, many plants and animals are unable to live anywhere else, like the little 'hairy-canary fly'! Many bog plants have turned carnivorous, so they get their five-a-day by munching on passing creepy-crawlies.

Peat bogs can throw up some amazing human artifacts as well. The remains of people who fell (or were pushed!) into the bogs several thousand years ago have been discovered, often still clothed, and so well preserved by our precious bogs that scientists have even been able to admire how beautifully they looked after their nails, how they wore their hair, and even what they had for supper! So, have a heart, don't rob the bog, use compost instead!

GLOSSARY

Anthers the male part of the flower which holds the pollen.

Arthropod an animal with no backbone but with an external skeleton and with many legs, for example, spiders, insects woodlice and crabs.

Carbon dioxide gas that plants use in photosynthesis but that is damaging to the environment in high quantities.

Chlorophyll the green substance in plants that stores the sun's energy.

Chemical a substance that can be good or bad and can be mixed together to make other substances.

Chrysalis the third stage in the butterfly or moths life during which it transforms from a caterpillar (also called the larva) into a butterfly or moth. The chrysalis is also called the pupa and it describes the hard bean shaped case inside which the transformation takes place.

Climate the regular weather conditions of an area.

Cocoon a silken purse which a moth caterpillar spins around itself in order to protect itself as it pupates. Also used to describe the silk sack which a spider spins to protect her eggs.

Companion plants plants that help other plants.

Compost soil made from the decayed remains of kitchen and garden waste.

Crepuscular an animal who is active at dawn and dusk.

Cross-pollination when different varieties of plants pollinate each other.

Cycle a pattern of events that goes round and round.

Decayed rotted.

Diurnal an animal who is active during the day.

Eco-friendly products or methods of doing things that will not harm the world.

Ecosystem a collection of habitats and the creatures that live in them that all work together in a healthy and sustainable way.

Entomologist a person who studies insects and other arthropods.

Ericaceous a type of soil that is needed by blueberries and other acid-loving plants.

Evaporation the process where water changes from a liquid to a gas (water vapor).

Exhale to breathe out.

Flowers the part of a plant designed to make seeds.

Gas a substance that is not liquid or solid at room temperature.

Germination the time when a seed splits open and turns into a plant.

Habitat a place that gives living things the conditions that they need to live.

Hibernaculum the structure in which an animal hibernates.

Hibernate to go into a sleepy state in the colder months of the year so not to have to find food.

Honeydew a sweet, sticky liquid made by aphids and other insects.

Inhale to breathe in.

Insects six legged arthropods.

Invasive a plant that will produce so many roots or new plants that it becomes a pest.

Invertebrate an animal who has no internal skeleton, but has a hard outer skeleton instead, for example, a shell.

Leaves the parts of a plant designed to conduct photosynthesis.

Mammal warm-blooded animal that gives birth to live young and feeds them with milk.

Micro-organisms tiny creatures that need a magnifying glass or micro-scope to be seen.

Mould a fungus that grows on plants (and other surfaces). Usually harmful.

Mulch a layer of material, natural or man made, that covers an area of soil.

Nectar a sugary liquid made by flowers to attract pollinators.

Nitrogen an element found in the air and the soil that is necessary for plant growth.

Nocturnal animals that are active at night.

Nutrients plant foods, available naturally in the soil or in home-made or bought fertilizers.

Organic in gardening it is used to mean anything that doesn't contain harmful (especially man-made chemicals).

Ovary the female part of the flower that holds the ovules.

Ovules the female cell that will turn into a seed once it is fertilized.

Oxygen a gas that is essential to life.

Parasite a plant or animal that gains its nourishment from the living body of another plant or animal.

Peat a type of soil made from decayed plants.

Peat-free any type of soil which does not contain any peat. The only type to buy.

Petal the outer part of a flower, often brightly coloured to attract pollinators.

Photosynthesis a process carried out in the leaves of plants that is essential for all life on earth where the sun's energy is changed into oxygen and food.

Pollen the male cell that will combine with the female ovule to make a seed.

Prey animals who are eaten by other animals.

Pupa in butterflies and moths the pupa is the same as the chrysalis. In other insects such as ants and bees, the pupa or pupal stage is the third stage of their lives.

Reptiles cold blooded creatures, usually with scaly skin.

Seed dispersal the different methods used by plants to spread their seeds around.

Seeds the fertilized part of a plant that is designed to grow into a new plant.

Shoots the growing tips of stems or branches.

Stem the thin trunk or branches of a plant.

Stickle jar a large jam jar with a string tied securely around the neck, and looped underneath to make it safe and easy to carry.

Stigma the surface at the top of the style to which pollen sticks.

Style the female part of a flower that supports the stigma.

INDEX

DEDICATION AND THANKS

This book is dedicated to Mark, my lovely husband, and to Issy, my terrific daughter. Thank you for always being ready and willing to help with bug safaris, fungus forays and midnight mouse hunts and for all your invaluable suggestions and encouragement.

Thank you also to Toby, my boy, for constructing bat boxes and hibernaculums and for buckets-full of expert advice. Thank-you to Bex and Mum and to Wendy, my best friend, for all your frank and helpful advice and support. Thanks, as always, to Alice, and also to Izzy, Georgia, Eddie, Will and Lois, to the children of Chalford Hill School gardening club, to Marcus, Luke and Emma and to Mr Burn at Thomas Keble School for allowing me to photograph the wildlife in the pond.

A special mention and thanks go to Serena and all the terrific people at the Oak and Furrows Wildlife Rescue Centre near Cirencester for allowing me to stand and watch the experts at work and for answering my endless questions with patient good-humour.

Thanks also to Duncan and to Alex for your wonderful design work and unfailing patience and to Stella for interpreting my thoughts so perfectly into your super drawings.

Elizabeth McCorquodale

Credits:
p. 64 courtesy Benny Mazur (Water spider)
p. 64 courtesy Doctor Swan (Caddis fly)
p. 72 courtesy Lip Kee (Swallow top)
p. 80 courtesy SiLVeR-13 (Fox cubs)
p. 82 courtesy Michael Spiller (Bat top)
p. 82 courtesy Ken Bosma (Bat bottom)
p. 88 courtesy Ingrid Taylar (Waxwing, top left)

Black Dog Publishing Limited
10a Acton Street
London WC1X 9NG
United Kingdom
info@blackdogonline.com

Edited and designed by Black Dog Publishing, London, UK. Illustrations by Stella Macdonald.

ISBN 978 1 907317 20 0

British Library Cataloguing-in-Publication Data. A CIP record for this book is available from the British Library.

Black Dog Publishing Limited, London, UK, is an environmentally responsible company. **Kids in the Wild Garden** is printed on an FSC certified paper.

Printed in China by Everbest Printing Co. Ltd

architecture art design
fashion history photography
theory and things

www.blackdogonline.com

london uk